Gathering the Pieces

A MEMOIR

By

LENNIE CAMPBELL

ISBN: 979-8-9992432-0-1 (Paperback)
ISBN: 979-8-9992432-1-8 (eBook)
ISBN: 979-8-9992432-2-5 (Hardcover)

Cover illustration and design by Lennie Campbell

Book layout design by Wordxense

www.gatheringthepieces.com

Website design by Ayomide

Email: ayomideoyinkansola88@gmail.com

Published by: Lantern Light Press, USA

Printed in the United States of America

First Edition

This is a true story, told to the best of the author's memory. Names and identifying details have been changed in certain instances to protect privacy. Some dialogue has been reconstructed or compressed for clarity and narrative flow.

For permissions, interviews or inquiries, contact the author:

lennie@gatheringthepieces.com

Dedication

For my son,
whose life changed mine forever
and whose absence I carry in every beat of my heart.

For my mother,
who left too soon,
but whose love lives on in everything I've ever done right.

For my father,
my hero and best friend,
who left too soon, but whom I carry with me forever.

For my sister,
whose sudden loss cut deep,
and through that pain I found words to finish this book.

Preface

THERE ARE STORIES WE CARRY IN SILENCE — memories too fragile or too painful to bring into the light. This book began as one of those stories.

For most of my life, I believed my past had to remain hidden. The pain. The shame. The silence. I learned how to smile through grief, to succeed in the shadow of survival, and to carry on without ever truly being seen. But healing, I discovered, isn't about forgetting or covering what's broken — it's about turning toward it, piece by piece, and daring to build something new.

Gathering the Pieces is the true story of how I did just that.

It isn't a straight line. There are sharp turns, devastating losses, hard truths, and unexpected moments of grace. There are scenes I never thought I'd share — and yet, in writing them, I found freedom. I found connection. I found the quiet strength that comes from telling the truth, even when your voice shakes.

This book is for anyone who has ever had to begin again. For those who have stood at the edge of themselves, unsure if they could go on. For those still gathering their own pieces, I offer mine — not as a guide, but as a hand held open in recognition.

Thank you for walking this path with me.
— *Lennie Campbell*

Table of Contents

For those who've had to start over—
And for those still gathering their pieces.

Chapter 1
The Heart of Home

Our house was never quiet.

The walls seemed to hum with life—footsteps pounding down the stairs, laughter bursting from the kitchen, the occasional crash of something tipping over.

It was the sound of everything I thought would always be there.

Every morning was a flurry of activity, voices overlapping, feet racing down the halls, laughter colliding with the sound of clattering dishes.

There were five of us—two boys, three girls—and I was the caboose at the end of the line. The youngest. I learned to read the room before I could read books, to find quiet in the corners of chaos. Our home sang with energy, and I was born into its melody.

It was a symphony of life—messy, loud, and beautiful.

I was very young then—maybe five.

Small enough that the doorknob felt high in my hand and the world seemed full of things just out of reach.

My oldest sister Alice's bedroom always felt like a world I wasn't quite old enough to enter.

She kept her door slightly ajar, just enough to stir my curiosity. I only ever stepped inside when she was gone for the day—at school or off with friends—when the house felt a little quieter, and I could slip into her room unnoticed.

On her neatly made bed sat a porcelain doll—poised and perfect, with glassy blue eyes and golden curls that never moved. She wore a delicate pink dress with lace trim and shiny shoes that never scuffed. That doll felt like royalty to me, untouched and far too precious for my small hands.

Very carefully, I'd walk up to the bed and look at the doll, standing only inches from her.

I never dared to touch her—just looked, heart pounding a little, as if the doll might know I was there.

Her stuffed animals—big ones her boyfriends had won for her at the county fair—sat on the floor along one wall, propped up like silent giants. I had to pass them to get to the bed, their plush arms flopped outward, their button eyes catching the light as I moved through the room.

They seemed to watch me, making the whole space feel even more grown-up, more off-limits, more magical.

Her room felt orderly, calm, almost sacred. It was the opposite of mine, where chaos reigned and toys spilled from every corner.

I don't remember ever asking permission to enter.

Just being close—just seeing it—felt like enough.

The Rhythm of Mornings

Mornings always followed a familiar rhythm.

The sizzle of bacon in the pan.

The gurgle of the coffee pot.

The shuffle of slippered feet against the hardwood floor.

Each sound signaled the start of a new day.

The smell of bacon and fresh coffee drifted from the kitchen, wrapping the whole house in warmth and comfort.

Mom, with her ever-present smile, moved gracefully between the stove and kitchen table, balancing a spatula in one hand and a plate in the other.

The clatter of dishes and the hum of conversation provided the soundtrack to our mornings.

Dad sat at the head of the table, a steady presence behind a cup of coffee and the morning newspaper.

His calmness anchored our chaos, reminding us that all was well.

The Strength of My Parents

Once we rushed off to school, Mom transformed.

She would head to Dad's dental practice, slipping seamlessly into the role of the cheerful receptionist.

It always amazed me how she balanced her nurturing spirit with sharp wit and efficiency.

She had once been a promising nursing student, studying in the same building where Dad earned his dentistry degree.

They met there—a love story that began among textbooks and clinical labs.

Though she set aside her nursing dreams when our family blossomed, she never lost the warmth and care that made her the heart of our home.

Dad was our rock.

No matter how long his day had been, he always found time for us.

Tossing a football in the backyard.

Sitting on the porch, listening to our stories.

Laughing at our antics, no matter how tired he was.

His steady presence made our home a place of safety and comfort.

Weekends & Family Adventures

Weekends were magical.

After chores were done, the house transformed into a lively gathering place.

Friends and family would stop by, filling every room with laughter.

One summer stands out vividly—our family vacation in Penticton, Canada.

The whole family piled into the car, the journey itself as memorable as the destination.

At the hotel pool, Dad put on a show.

Dressed in one of Mom's oversized muumuus, he climbed onto the diving board, waving dramatically as he called her name.

Then, with surprising grace, he dove into the water.

The splash sent ripples of laughter around the pool.

Mom laughed, her eyes glinting with amusement—and a playful promise of revenge.

A Small Town Full of Magic

Growing up in a small rural town had its own kind of magic.

Mornings were crisp, with fog hanging low over the nut orchards.

Evenings smelled sweet as the sun dipped behind the fields.

The town proudly bore the name "Garden Spot," home to the largest dahlia grower in the United States.

Rows upon rows of dahlias stretched across the land like a vibrant, quilted blanket.

Bright reds, soft pinks, and deep purples danced in the breeze—a sight so ordinary then, yet pure magic in memory.

Three rivers ran through our town. They met at a state park—our park.

It was where we swam on hot summer days, skipping rocks until our arms were sore.

Where we lay on the grassy banks, watching clouds drift overhead.

We built forts in the brush, dared each other to explore deeper into the woods.

On those long summer days, life felt infinite.

As kids, we worked in the berry and bean fields for extra cash.

Our fingers were stained purple and red, our bellies full from sneaking bites.

We'd head straight to the five-and-dime with coins jingling in our pockets.

Penny candy lined the shelves—taffy, jawbreakers, licorice—little treasures waiting to be claimed.

The wooden floors creaked beneath us. The shopkeeper always greeted us by name.

Phones weren't private then—you shared the party line.

You might lift the receiver and find two neighbors already mid-conversation.

It could be annoying, but that was life—simple and connected.

And then there was the fair.

It wasn't just an event—it was the event of the year.

The Ferris wheel towered above everything, glowing in the night sky.

But for me, it was always about barrel racing.

My sister and I started small—Shetland ponies, ribbons flapping, dust rising.

The cheers from the crowd, the scent of hay and carnival rides in the air.

And always—my father's proud smile in the stands.

These moments—the laughter, the adventure, the sense of belonging—they shaped me.

We didn't know we were making memories.

We just thought we were living.

They were the heartbeat of a home I thought would never change.

At the time, I thought this life would last forever—the laughter, the routine, the comfort of my parents' love.

I didn't know that in a blink, everything would change.

And I would spend the rest of my life trying to gather the pieces.

Chapter 2
The Day the World Tilted

We never know when life will change.

Sometimes it happens slowly, with small shifts so subtle we hardly notice.

Other times, it crashes in all at once—loud, jarring, impossible to ignore.

For us, it came like a storm gathering on the horizon, dark clouds rolling in before we even had time to prepare.

The hum of everyday life continued—work, laughter around the dinner table.

But somewhere beneath it all, a change was coming.

And soon, it would sweep everything away.

The Last Ordinary Day

It was a beautiful, sunny day.

July 5th.

The brilliance of the Fourth of July had faded, leaving behind the lingering scent of fireworks and the quiet hum of summer.

I was babysitting that day, the sun streaming through the window, filling the room with warmth and light.

It felt like a day of possibility, of hope.

The warmth of the afternoon wrapped around me.

The scent of summer air drifted in through the screen door.

The kids were laughing.

The world was still.

And then—

The ring of the phone.

A sound so sharp, so sudden, that it sliced through the stillness.

Just the ordinary sound of a telephone.

Just another moment in an ordinary day.

Until it wasn't.

I picked it up.

"Hello?"

My oldest brother's voice came through the line, but something was wrong.

His tone was different—strained, unfamiliar.

The words came fast, disjointed. Urgent.

And then, the last thing he said before I dropped the phone:

"Run home. Run home as fast as you can."

I barely registered the knock at the door before a family friend stepped inside, taking my place with the children.

My legs carried me.

My heart pounded.

And I ran.

A Childhood of Steady Presence

My childhood was filled with warmth, security, and love.

We were a family of seven—three girls, two boys, and parents who were the center of our world.

We belonged to each other, tied together by laughter, summer vacations, and a bond that felt unbreakable.

Looking back, it all seemed too perfect before that moment.

Everything about our home, our life, felt solid.

The smell of Dad's aftershave when he kissed us goodnight.

The way he always knew how to fix anything—broken toys, skinned knees, bad days.

The sound of his steady voice, telling stories, offering advice, reminding us that we were safe.

He had been our foundation.

The man who made everything feel stable, unshakable.

And then, in an instant, that foundation was gone.

The Day the World Tilted

I don't remember much about the run home, only that my feet barely touched the pavement.

As I approached our house, everyone was outside, waiting.

Their faces were tight.

Their postures rigid.

The air felt wrong, thick with something I couldn't name.

Then, the words.

The ones that changed everything.

My father had been at a council meeting, standing before a room full of men.

He was not just a man in our town—he was the man.

The mayor. The leader.

The one people turned to for strength, for answers.

He was steady.

Reliable.

He was my father.

My hero.

And then, in an instant,

He was gone.

A heart attack.

No warnings.

No goodbyes.

The Hospital and My Mother's Plea

The hospital was thirty-five minutes away, but it might as well have been another world.

We arrived in a blur of movement—my mother rushing from the car, us scrambling behind her.

The bright hospital lights were harsh, sterile. The halls smelled of antiseptic and something heavier, something final.

"Mrs. Guile... Mrs. Guile..."

The nurses caught her before she could reach him, their hands soft but firm, their faces filled with something I didn't want to understand.

"We need to change his diet."

Mom continued, her voice trembling but insistent.

"We need to change his diet. We'll get him to eat healthier. He just needs to eat better. We'll take walks every evening—he'll get stronger. He just needs time. Just time."

Her hands clutched at the nurse's sleeve, gripping like a lifeline, as if sheer determination could reverse what had already happened.

"Please... we'll fix it. I promise. We'll fix it."

But the nurses only looked at her with soft, knowing eyes, their silence heavier than any words.

She shook her head, refusing to hear it. Refusing to let go.

"He just needs more time," she whispered, almost to herself.

But time had already run out.

The words hung in the air, surreal and impossible.

My body refused to move, as if by standing still, I could hold the world together for just a moment longer—for me, for my brother and sisters, for my mother.

But they were already shaking their heads.

He was gone.

The world tilted that day.

One moment, I was a girl lying under the stars with her father, dreaming about life.

The next, I was fourteen years old and fatherless.

The House Without Him

The laughter in our house drained away overnight.

The air became heavy, thick with something we didn't know how to process.

The backyard, once my sanctuary, became a hollow place—too quiet, too still.

I kept waiting.

Waiting for his voice.

Waiting for the sound of his footsteps.

Waiting for the impossible—to wake up and find it had all been a terrible mistake.

But he never came home.

A Town in Mourning

The town mourned him.

Flags flew at half-staff.

In the days leading up to the funeral, people looked at us in a certain way—a mix of pity and disbelief.

They tried to find the right words, offering condolences, telling us how sorry they were for our loss, speaking of a man who had been so strong, so respected.

They all meant well, but in my heart, none of it changed the truth.

My dad was gone.

The Taps Rang Out

The first note of Taps rang out, sharp and final.

The flag was folded with crisp precision, each movement sharp and deliberate.

I watched as the white-gloved hands of the officer pressed the edges together, tucking them tightly — transforming the fabric into a perfect triangle.

My mother sat still, her hands clasped in her lap, her face pale but composed.

When the officer knelt before her, his voice was steady, rehearsed.

"On behalf of the President of the United States, the United States Navy, and a grateful nation, please accept this flag as a symbol of our appreciation for your loved one's honorable and faithful service."

She reached out, taking the flag with both hands, her fingers trembling as she pressed it to her chest.

It was a symbol of honor, of duty, of sacrifice.

Navy Lieutenant. War Veteran. Mayor. Dentist. Husband. Father.

The man who had once worn that uniform with pride, who had returned from World War II and put himself through dental school by driving a taxi—He was gone.

And no flag, no carefully spoken words, could fill the void he left behind.

A gust of wind stirred the trees as silence settled over the crowd.

Then, from a short distance away, the sharp, sorrowful sound of Taps began.

The first note hit like a punch to my chest.

I gritted my teeth as the melody carried over the graves, slow and aching, each note stretching through the stillness, each pause carving deeper into the emptiness he had left behind.

The final note hung in the air before dissolving into silence.

I swallowed hard.

This was it.

This was goodbye.

And then came the shovels.

One by one, they began to lower scoops of dirt onto the casket.

I was standing just a few feet away, watching the earth fall—each thud louder than the last.

It hit me like a wave—seeing the dirt cover the polished wood: the last visible part of my father being buried.

My knees buckled.

The world tilted again.

I started to fall.

Hands caught me—someone yelling my name.

They rushed to get smelling salts.

I hadn't realized I had stopped breathing until the rush of sharp ammonia hit my nose and brought me back.

I was fourteen.

And I had just watched my hero be lowered into the ground.

We had driven behind the hearse in a long procession, moving through the road leading to the cemetery. People had lined the sides of the road, removing their hats, standing still in silent respect. The town had lost a leader.

But we had lost the man who taught us how to be strong.

How could I say goodbye to the man who pointed out constellations in the night sky?

Who made us laugh, who filled our home with stories? The man who had always been the steady foundation beneath us?

I looked at my siblings, at my mother, at the polished wooden casket draped in the American flag.

And I knew that from this moment on, nothing would ever be the same.

The world had moved forward.

But I felt frozen, standing on the edge of a life that no longer included my father.

Throughout the entire funeral procession there was one thing missing.

My brother, James.

The third child in our family.

He wasn't here.

Not because he didn't want to be, but because he couldn't be.

The Navy had done everything they could to get him home in time, but the ocean is vast, and time doesn't slow for grief.

The call had gone out. Orders had been pulled. But there were limits, even in emergencies.

He was arriving in 48 hours.

The grave had already been filled.

The flag had already been folded.

The final words had already been spoken.

While we stood at the cemetery that day, saying goodbye, he was somewhere out on the water—knowing, but not being there.

And that loss—the loss of saying goodbye, of standing with his family, of having a final moment with our father—stayed with him.

Grief is heavy, but grief with regret is unbearable.

Chapter 3
James's Tragic Homecoming

When James finally came home, the house felt different. The front door creaked as he stepped inside, the familiar scent of wood polish and my mother's lingering perfume filling the air. But the house didn't feel like home anymore. It felt hollow. As if it had inhaled all of our grief and was now holding its breath, waiting for someone to exhale first.

There were no more guests bringing food, no more whispered condolences. The funeral was already past. Life had already moved forward.

But for James, time had stopped the moment he got the call at sea.

I watched him as he stood in the entryway, his duffel bag slung over one shoulder, his uniform wrinkled from the long trip home. His eyes, usually sharp and full of life, were dull now, lost in something far away.

He set his bag down carefully, like the floor beneath him was fragile, like everything in his world could shatter at the slightest touch.

I wanted to say something.

But what do you say to someone who missed his own father's funeral?

What do you say to a brother who wasn't there to say goodbye?

I glanced at the coat rack, where a dusty old fishing hat still hung— Dad's favorite one. The sight of it hit me like a stone. I remembered the quiet mornings James used to spend with Dad, casting lines into the lake just as the sun rose, sharing thermoses of coffee and stories that never made it back to the rest of us. That was their time.

And now, Dad was gone.

And James never got to say goodbye.

The Weight of a Missed Goodbye

James didn't talk much that first night.

He sat in Dad's old chair in the living room, staring at the floor. The rest of us moved around him, setting the table for dinner, pretending this was normal. Pretending like Dad wasn't missing from his usual spot at the head of the table.

"Everyone was at the house, offering support—to Mom, to each other, and to themselves."

I watched my mother set a plate in front of James, her hands trembling slightly as she placed the silverware beside it. It was the same way she had set a plate for Dad after he died, as if muscle memory couldn't let her forget he was gone.

James barely touched his food. He chewed slowly, mechanically, swallowing without tasting.

At one point, Alice tried to fill the silence.

"I still can't believe how many people came to the service," she said softly.

"The church was packed, James."

A city council member spoke about Dad—about his leadership, his dedication to the town. Even the governor sent flowers."

James nodded but didn't look up.

I knew what he was thinking.

It didn't matter how many people were there.

He wasn't.

The Ride That Changed Everything

The next morning, James barely spoke. He disappeared into the garage after breakfast, emerging hours later with his old motorcycle keys in hand.

Mom tensed when she saw him.

"You sure that's a good idea?" she asked, her voice thin with worry.

James just shrugged. "I need to clear my head."

He needed to breathe, I thought. To escape the weight of a home that no longer felt like his.

I watched as he wheeled the bike onto the driveway, his movements slow and deliberate, as if he was reacquainting himself with something familiar.

The bike had sat untouched for months. The tires were still caked with dust. But when he turned the key, the engine roared to life, splitting the quiet morning air.

Without another word, he swung his leg over and sped off down the street.

I watched him disappear, a tight knot forming in my stomach.

I had a bad feeling.

I told myself it was nothing—just the fear of someone I loved taking off too soon, too fast.

But I was wrong.

That was the last time I saw James before the accident.

The Crash

The sun had started to set when the phone rang.

I was in the kitchen, clearing plates from the sink.

Mom picked up the phone. I heard the sharp intake of her breath. The way the dish towel in her hand slipped to the floor.

Then, her voice—shaky, thin.

"Oh God," she whispered.

The words barely made it past her lips.

I stopped breathing.

Alice, who had been helping me, froze mid-motion, a plate still in her hand.

"What?" I whispered. "What is it?"

Mom's grip tightened around the phone.

"It's James," she said. "There's been an accident."

The words rang through the kitchen, bouncing off the walls, ricocheting inside my head.

Accident.

James.

No.

Not again.

At the Hospital

The drive to the hospital was a blur. My mother gripped the steering wheel so tightly her knuckles turned white.

When we got there, the smell of antiseptic burned my nose, the too-bright fluorescent lights making everything feel harsh and unnatural.

James lay in a hospital bed, wrapped in white.

His legs elevated, his arms locked in place, his head bandaged, a tracheotomy in his throat.

I stared at him, my stomach churning. The machine beside him beeped rhythmically, a cruel reminder that this was real.

Mom gasped when she saw him, covering her mouth with trembling fingers.

I took a step forward, but my knees felt weak.

He looked so small.

So breakable.

So unlike the brother who had roared down the driveway just that morning, chasing freedom.

The doctor met us with somber eyes.

"His injuries are extensive," he said gently. "Multiple fractures. Internal bleeding. We've done everything we can. Now, we just wait for the swelling to subside. In a week we will need to apply a full body cast."

Wait.

That's all we could do.

So, we waited.

We sat beside him, watching the slow rise and fall of his chest, praying for him to wake up.

A Sign of Life

Days passed.

James didn't move.

Didn't wake.

And then, one afternoon, something happened.

James. He was moving.

He blinked, groggy, disoriented.

Then—he opened his mouth.

His gaze darted around the room, confused, frantic.

And then—his hand reached toward the bedside table.

There was a small bar of soap sitting there.

Before I could stop him—

He took a bite.

"James!" I yelped, jumping up.

A nurse rushed in, gently prying the soap from his hand.

His eyes were glassy, unfocused. He thought it was cheese.

The Road to Recovery

James had a long fight ahead of him.

And so did we.

But as I sat beside him that night, listening to the rhythmic beeping of the machines, I made a silent promise.

We had lost Dad.

But we wouldn't lose him.

Not now.

Not ever.

I didn't know what the road ahead would look like—or how long it would take—but I knew one thing for sure: we would walk it together.

But taking care of James meant my mother had to make an impossible choice—

And that's how I ended up at St. Agnes.

Chapter 4
St. Agnes

S t. Agnes Academy for girls loomed in front of me as we drove down the long, winding driveway. The building was imposing, its stone exterior weathered by time, giving it an almost fortress-like presence. Ivy clung stubbornly to parts of the walls, weaving through cracks and creeping toward the high, arched windows that reflected the gray sky above. The towering structure stretched endlessly toward the sky. The gravel beneath the tires crunched as we slowed to a stop in front of the concrete staircase leading to the entrance.

I stared up at the massive structure, my stomach twisting into knots. "This is where I'm going to live for nine months," I murmured, more to myself than to my mother.

"I'll come get you for the next few weekends, and after that, your sister will come pick you up. You can spend time with her."

She was talking about my oldest sister, Alice. She was ten years older and worked for a stock brokerage firm in the city. I loved spending time with her there. Like Alice, my other brothers and sister no longer lived at home.

She turned to me, her expression a mixture of sadness and resolve. "Honey, I need you to be here," she said gently. "James still has a long road ahead of him. He needs me, and soon, I'll be going with him to Texas, to a veterans' facility for rehabilitation. He needs to learn how to walk again and strengthen his entire body."

I swallowed hard. I knew James had been through something unimaginable, but I couldn't help the bitterness that crept into my voice. "So, you're leaving too."

Mom reached over, brushing a loose strand of hair from my face. "It's not like that," she whispered. "I love you. This isn't forever."

I pulled away from her.

But it felt like it would be forever.

The car rolled to a stop, silence stretching between us. Mom reached for the trunk latch, the quiet click filling the space between us like a final goodbye. She stepped out, moving quickly around the car, lifting my suitcase from the trunk as if hurrying would somehow make this easier.

I didn't move right away. My fingers clenched the seat beneath me, my chest tight. This was really happening.

"Come on, honey. I'll call you in a few days after you've had a chance to get settled," she said gently, her voice strained. "And you can always call me for the next few weeks. Let's go."

It would be a long-distance call for me to call home. That had been discussed with Mom ahead of time, and I had money to use the Academy's pay phone.

I opened the car door and stepped onto the gravel driveway. The scent of damp earth and fresh-cut grass filled my nose, grounding me for just a second before the wave of reality hit me again. I was here. And I wouldn't be leaving anytime soon.

We climbed the wide steps together, the sound of our shoes tapping against the hard surface echoing in my ears. Up close, the building felt even more intimidating—tall, heavy, and unyielding. The stone walls seemed to absorb the light, making the entranceway feel shadowed despite the open sky above. The thick iron railings lining the steps were cold to the touch, their chill sinking into my fingertips. As we ascended, the massive arched windows loomed above us like watchful eyes, their glass panes clouded by time and weather.

The entrance doors were made of heavy, dark wood, their surface worn smooth from years of use. Deep grooves and ornate carvings decorated the panels, giving them an almost medieval feel. The brass handles gleamed dully in the fading light, their edges darkened by countless hands that had grasped them before me. They stood tall and unyielding, like a gateway to another world. Standing at the top, waiting for us, were two nuns dressed in full black habits, their long veils flowing down their backs, their black shoes barely visible beneath the heavy fabric. Their expressions were unreadable, their hands folded neatly in front of them as if they had been expecting me.

As we reached the last step, they greeted us with a formal nod. My mother, her voice soft but steady, introduced me. "This is Ellen."

The nuns simply gave another nod, their faces calm, composed, impassive. Then, in a tone as solemn as their expressions, one of them finally spoke.

"Welcome, Ellen." The words felt heavy, final. Not warm, not cruel— just an acknowledgment, as if I had stepped across an invisible threshold into a world where I no longer had a say.

A flicker of defiance flared in me. They didn't know me. They didn't know what I had already been through.

They hadn't watched my father lowered into the ground. They hadn't sat beside James in the hospital and made a silent promise to hold the rest of it together.

If they thought I was just another quiet, obedient girl, they were wrong. Their voices were measured, emotionless, like they had said these words a hundred times before. I lifted my chin just slightly, refusing to let them see how much I wanted to disappear. If they thought I would break easily, they were wrong. The single word was not warm, nor was it cold— it simply was, a formal acknowledgment of my arrival, as if I had just stepped into a world where emotion had no place. Their presence, though silent, felt authoritative, like sentinels guarding the threshold between my old life and whatever waited beyond those wooden doors.

Mom turned to me, her eyes filled with something I couldn't name. She handed me my suitcase, her fingers lingering for a brief second before she gave me a quick, tight hug, then pulled away.

Without another word, she turned and walked down the steps toward the car. I wanted to call out, to demand that she take me with her, but my throat clenched shut. Instead, I stood still, gripping my suitcase so tightly my fingers ached, watching as she climbed into the driver's seat.

My chest tightened, my breath shallow. The reality of it all hit me—Dad was gone, James was struggling to survive, and now, Mom was leaving too. It wasn't fair. None of it was. A knot of rebellion coiled in my stomach, a silent, stubborn refusal to fully accept what was happening.

The engine hummed to life. The tires crunched over gravel as the car backed away. I stood there, staring at the space where it had been, my body tense with the weight of everything left unsaid. The air felt heavier now, pressing against my chest, as if the very world had conspired to trap me here. Just like that, she was gone.

I turned back toward the nuns, my suitcase feeling heavier than it had moments before. Something inside me twisted—grief, anger, defiance, all tangled together. My father had just died. My mother was leaving. And now, these strangers in black robes were all that remained. The thought made me clench my jaw, a quiet rebellion burning inside me.

Without a word, they stepped aside, gesturing for me to follow. The doors loomed before me, dark and heavy, the worn brass handle cold under my palm. I took one last breath of the outside air before stepping forward. If I had to be here, I would do it my way—silent, watchful, waiting for my moment.

If this place thought it could break me, it had no idea who it was dealing with.

It would not break me.

It never would.

Not after everything I'd already been through.

Not after holding my breath beside my brother's hospital bed.

Not after standing graveside as the world tilted beneath me.

This place might silence me, might press against every edge of who I was—but it would not undo me.

Even here, I would hold on to myself.

Chapter 5
The Tour of St. Agnes

The heavy wooden doors of St. Agnes Academy closed behind me with a dull finality, sealing me into this unfamiliar world. It sounded like a sigh. Or maybe a warning. Either way, there was no going back.

The cool air inside smelled of polished wood and faint lemon-scented cleaner. The hall stretched out before me, lined with religious paintings and statues that seemed to watch my every move.

Sister Amelia Ann turned toward me with a nod.

"This way," she instructed, her voice even, giving nothing away.

I followed her, my footsteps muffled against the worn wooden floors. The hallways were dim, the only light filtering in from the tall, narrow windows spaced between the framed depictions of saints and biblical scenes. Each corner we turned revealed more of the same—long, quiet corridors that carried the faintest whispers of past conversations, now long gone.

The tour continued through the dining hall, where rows of wooden tables stood in perfect alignment, waiting for the students to arrive. A crucifix hung on the far wall, overlooking the room, its presence unavoidable.

"Dinner will be at five sharp tonight and breakfast is at seven sharp in the morning."

I swallowed, nodding.

Next, we passed the chapel, its arched doorway revealing a space bathed in colored light from the stained-glass windows. The scent of burning wax and aged incense clung to the air, mixing with the faint chill that always seemed to linger inside.

The high, vaulted ceiling loomed above, making the space feel grand yet oppressive, like it was watching over us. The wooden pews stretched in long, orderly rows, their surfaces smooth but unforgiving. No cushion. No comfort. Just polished wood that forced perfect posture.

At the front, a large statue of the Virgin Mary stood in silent grace, her eyes cast downward, her hands open in quiet acceptance. The flickering candlelight played across her serene face, making the shadows shift and move, almost as if she were watching.

Dozens of burnt-out candles crowded the altar, their half-melted wax pooled in thick, uneven layers—the remnants of prayers whispered in hushed voices.

At that hour, the light through the stained-glass windows was soft and muted, casting pale blues, reds, and golds across the stone floor.

The nuns expected silence. Reverence. Heads bowed. Hands folded. But my eyes always wandered—to the swirling colors on the walls, to the high ceiling where dust floated in the air, to the candle flames that danced and flickered, alive in the stillness.

It was beautiful.

But it wasn't warm.

It felt like a place where grief was expected to be silent.

And I would come to know that silence well. Every Wednesday morning at six, I sat stiffly in one of those pews, the air thick with incense and Latin prayers I couldn't understand. The priest would swing the censer, the sweet, smoky scent growing stronger with each pass until it turned my empty stomach inside out. I wasn't Catholic, but it didn't matter. All the girls—no matter their age, no matter their faith—were required to attend. We sat there in the dim chill of morning, heads bowed, trying not to sway from exhaustion or nausea, trying to make sense of words that meant nothing to us. It felt more like endurance than reverence. More like obedience than faith.

As we walked past, I felt the cool air drift from inside, brushing against my skin like a whisper of something unseen.

"This is where you will attend Mass on Wednesday mornings before breakfast," Sister Amelia Ann explained.

I hesitated. "I'm not Catholic," I admitted quietly.

Her gaze flicked to me, unreadable. "Then you will observe and learn."

My stomach tightened. I bit the inside of my cheek, already understanding that resistance here wouldn't get me far.

There was no room for discussion.

At that moment I longed to be home with my friends, in a place that was familiar.

Sister Theresa met us in the hallway and led me up the wide, creaking staircase to the second floor, her black habit swishing softly with each step.

I didn't know it then, but Sister Theresa would become the quiet center in a place that often felt harsh. She was the softest spoken of all the nuns—gentle, kind, and always a little less severe in her expectations.

Sister Amelia Ann, on the other hand, was the dean of girls—and from day one, we were at odds.

She was stoic, rule-bound, and quick to call my mother about my antics. She was the one who kept me at the school on weekends to scrub floors and wash Venetian blinds. We clashed in ways I wasn't yet ready to understand—but the tension between us was only just beginning.

The air grew cooler as we ascended, carrying the faint scent of old wood and floor polish. My heartbeat quickened—not from exertion, but from the growing realization that this was where I would sleep, live, and exist for the next nine months.

We entered the dormitory, and I hesitated in the doorway.

Fifteen identical beds stretched in two straight rows, each separated by thin beige curtains that swayed slightly with the draft from the hallway. They offered only the illusion of privacy—thin barriers between whispered conversations and restless sleep.

The blankets were stiff and scratchy, a dull shade of grayish-blue, folded neatly at the foot of each bed. The pillows looked barely thick enough to provide comfort, flattened from years of use.

The walls, painted a muted off-white, absorbed the dim glow from the overhead fluorescent bulbs. The lights flickered faintly, emitting a low, crackling hum that blended with the occasional rustle of fabric or the distant echo of footsteps in the corridor. Against one wall, long Venetian blinds covered the windows, their slats slightly bent and coated in a thin layer of dust.

They rattled softly when the wind pressed against the panes, casting thin, horizontal shadows across the floor.

The dormitory felt sterile, rigid—like it belonged to another era, frozen in time. There was no warmth here, no signs of personal touch. Each bed was just another in a row, another space to sleep, another girl who had once been assigned to it and eventually left.

How many girls had cried themselves to sleep behind those thin curtains?

How many never let anyone hear them?

I exhaled slowly, feeling a strange sense of relief that I wouldn't be sleeping in this room. My semi-private room—while still foreign and unfamiliar—was at least a space I could call my own.

It wasn't much, but it was something.

As we moved out of the dormitory and further down the hallway, Sister Theresa continued walking, motioning for me to follow. As she turned a corner, she finally spoke, her voice even.

"This will be your room," she said, pushing the door open.

"You will have a roommate," she continued. "Claire Donnelly. She arrives tomorrow."

"Supper is at five."

And with that, she turned and walked away, leaving me standing in the long corridor alone.

The Room & The Balcony

The room was simple—two narrow beds with thin mattresses, their frames made of dark, polished wood. Two wooden dressers, scuffed from years of use, stood side by side, their handles slightly loose. A small desk was positioned beneath a tall window, its glass smudged from countless hands opening and closing it over the years.

The air smelled of old wood, mingled with something faintly medicinal, like freshly laundered linens and the lingering scent of floor polish. The wooden planks creaked slightly beneath my feet as I stepped further inside, the sound hollow in the quiet space.

A single, faded rug lay in the center of the floor, its once vibrant colors now dulled, its edges frayed from years of footsteps crossing over it. A modest bathroom was tucked into the corner, its mirror speckled with age, its porcelain sink showing fine cracks from time and wear.

But what caught my attention was the balcony.

I stepped toward it instinctively, my fingers brushing against the cool brass handle before pushing the door open. A rush of crisp, fresh air met me, carrying the scent of pine and damp earth.

The view stretched beyond the grounds, past the neatly trimmed hedges and the towering trees that framed the school. In the distance, the sky stretched endlessly, a soft wash of blue and gray, the clouds shifting in slow, steady waves.

The crisp scent of wood lingered in the air, stirring a memory deep inside me. I was suddenly back home, standing outside in the chill of autumn, my siblings and I gathered around a pile of smoldering leaves.

I could almost hear the crackling of the fire as we poked at the foil-wrapped apples nestled within the embers, their skins darkening, the cinnamon and sugar inside caramelizing into something warm and sweet. The anticipation, the laughter, the way we would huddle together, waiting for the perfect moment to peel back the foil and take that first bite—tart, sweet, and steaming hot against the cold air.

That memory was proof—I had once belonged somewhere.

The memory filled me with an ache I hadn't expected.

I blinked, shaking off the wave of nostalgia. That life felt so far away now.

Stepping back inside, I closed the balcony door behind me and let out a slow breath.

This was home now. At least for the next nine months.

But standing there, with the scent of wood and the bite of fresh air still clinging to my senses, I let myself hold onto the memory a little longer.

Just a little longer.

An Empty Dining Room & A Lonely Meal

That evening at five, I found myself alone in the large, stark dining hall, the sound of my footsteps swallowed by the vast emptiness of the space. The wooden chairs were tucked neatly under the long rows of tables, as if waiting for the other girls who would arrive the next day.

Sister Amelia Ann appeared, carrying a small bowl of soup, a glass of milk, and a slice of bread, placing them in front of me without a word.

I stared down at the meal—simple, plain, offering neither warmth nor comfort.

40

The silence pressed in, heavier than I had expected. No familiar voices. No laughter. No family.

Just me.

I picked up my spoon and took a slow sip of the chicken scup, its blandness settling into my stomach like the realization that I was truly alone here.

The only sound was the ticking of the old dining hall clock and the soft scrape of my spoon against the ceramic bowl.

Tomorrow couldn't come fast enough.

Tomorrow, this place would no longer be empty.

But tonight, I sat in the silence of everything I had lost.

And waited for something new to begin.

Chapter 6
The Hidden Room

The first time I really spoke to Anna, she found me in the one place I thought no one would.

The small chapel on the second floor was hidden—unmarked, unnoticed, and exactly what I needed. It had become my sanctuary in the short time I had been at St. Agnes—a place where I could escape the heavy silence of my dorm room, the endless rules, and the ache that followed me everywhere. Grief I wasn't allowed to name.

Inside, the chapel was unlike the rest of the school. Where the dorms and classrooms smelled of waxed floors and chalk dust, the chapel smelled of aged books, melted candle wax, and the faintest hint of incense. The stone walls held the coolness of the morning air, but the warmth of flickering candles cast long, golden shadows across the floor.

The stained-glass windows, depicting saints I didn't recognize, filtered the late afternoon sun into rich blues, greens, and fiery reds. It was the only place in the entire school that didn't feel old and heavy—it felt untouched, peaceful, like a secret world just for me.

I had curled up on one of the wooden pews, hugging my knees, letting the quiet wrap around me.

I sat alone, holding back tears, trying to make sense of why I was here.

St. Agnes was cold, quiet, unfamiliar. And even though I knew my mother had no place else to send me—or at least, believed she didn't—I couldn't help but feel the ache of abandonment.

James had just survived a horrific motorcycle accident.

She needed to be with him.

I understood that.

But understanding doesn't make the loneliness go away.

I missed my dad.

I missed my mom.

I missed my home.

And as much as I tried to stay strong, the tears came anyway—quiet at first, then slipping freely down my cheeks. I was grieving more than one thing in that moment: the loss of my father, yes, but also the loss of everything that had once felt safe and known.

And then—just as the tears fell—Anna stepped into the room.

"So, do you always sit in chapels looking dramatic, or is that just for effect?"

I nearly jumped out of my skin.

I turned sharply, my pulse racing, to find a girl leaning casually against the doorway, arms crossed, a smirk tugging at her lips.

I narrowed my eyes. "Excuse me?"

I hadn't heard footsteps. Hadn't expected anyone to find me here. The sudden intrusion shook something loose—my guard, maybe.

She stepped inside, her black school shoes clicking softly against the stone. "I've seen you slip in here before. Figured you were either praying or plotting something."

I let out a short laugh. "Maybe both."

She grinned, sliding into the pew across from me. The faint smell of peppermint gum followed her, and she moved with the ease of someone who didn't care what rules she broke. "I'm Anna."

She had dark, curly hair that framed her face in soft waves, striking blue eyes, and a mischievous smile that made it hard to tell whether she was teasing or telling the truth.

I studied her. She was different from the other girls—her uniform slightly rumpled, her sleeves pushed up as if she wasn't afraid of bending the rules. There was something about her that felt... safe.

She leaned back, tilting her head toward the ceiling. "So, what is it? Praying or plotting?"

I wanted to lie. To say I was just thinking, or bored, or anything else that didn't feel so raw. But something about her—her ease, her honesty—made me want to tell the truth.

I hesitated before answering. "Hiding."

She nodded, her expression shifting. "Yeah," she said, her voice softer now. "Me too."

A pause.

Then, she looked over at me again. "I heard about your dad."

I hadn't expected her to say that. The ache inside me had stayed so quiet for so long, I almost forgot how close to the surface it really was.

The words hit me like a punch to the chest. I felt my jaw tighten, my stomach twist. I hadn't talked about it. Not to anyone.

I swallowed hard. "Yeah."

"My dad died last year," she said, staring ahead at the stained-glass windows. "Cancer."

Silence stretched between us. Not awkward—just there.

I turned my gaze toward the colored light on the floor, unsure of what to say. Finally, I whispered. "I'm sorry."

She nodded. "Yeah. Me too."

And just like that, the weight I'd been carrying didn't feel quite so heavy.

We didn't say anything else after that. We didn't need to.

And in that moment, I knew—I had made a friend.

In a place where I felt invisible, someone had seen me.

I didn't know it then, but that moment in the hidden chapel was the beginning of a lifeline. Not just a friendship—but a reminder that I hadn't disappeared completely. Someone still saw me.

Chapter 7
The Habit Heist

I hadn't laughed in weeks. Not really. But something about Anna made it feel possible again.

The air was crisp that evening, carrying the scent of damp stone and pine as Anna and I strolled back toward the dormitories. The sky stretched dark above us, speckled with faint stars barely visible against the glow of the campus lights. Our shoes crunched softly against the gravel path, the sound blending with the distant hum of cicadas hidden in the trees.

Anna nudged me with her elbow, her voice playful. "So, do you always sit in chapels looking dramatic, or is that just for effect?"

I smirked, rolling my eyes. "It's called contemplation. You wouldn't understand."

She grinned. "Oh, I understand perfectly. I just happen to contemplate things while sneaking cookies from the kitchen. You should try it sometime."

I glanced at her, a twinkle forming in my eyes. "Are you suggesting we break the rules?"

She feigned innocence. "Would I ever do such a thing?"

We laughed, the sound warm against the cold night air. The laughter was unrestrained, wild in a way that felt like defiance—like a small rebellion against the rigid structure of St. Agnes. A silent understanding passed between us—an unspoken agreement that maybe, just maybe, this place wasn't going to be so terrible after all.

I had made a new friend.

Midnight at the Grotto

The idea started as a joke, whispered under the flickering dormitory lights when we were supposed to be asleep.

"Bet you wouldn't dare," Anna whispered, her eyes glinting with mischief.

She had just appeared at my door—quiet, expectant—just as we had planned.

"Oh, wouldn't I?" I shot back, grinning.

Anna had a way of pulling me into trouble. By now, it was almost routine.

She was from Los Angeles and carried a kind of reckless energy—a spark that burned against the dull, monotonous routine of St. Agnes's Academy. While I was still trying to keep my head down, still figuring out how to breathe within the rigid structure of the school, Anna seemed determined to break every rule just to see if anyone would stop her.

And tonight—the challenge was irresistible.

The mission?

Sneak into the laundry room, steal two of the nuns' habits, and run around the grotto at midnight.

"Like saints in rebellion," Anna had joked. "Or sinners in disguise."

The idea sounded wild. Irresponsible. Fun.

Unfamiliar, but exactly what I needed.

I wasn't trying to be difficult.

I wasn't acting out just for the sake of it.

It wasn't rebellion. It was survival disguised as laughter.

A way to breathe in a place where everything felt like holding your breath.

I was a fourteen-year-old girl who had just lost her father, been sent away from my home, my friends, everything I knew.

And if sneaking into the laundry room, stealing a habit, and laughing in the moonlight helped me feel normal again, even for a moment—then I wasn't going to apologize for it.

The Heist

The school fell silent after lights out.

The ticking of the dorm clock felt louder with every passing second.

I could hear the soft breaths of the other girls sleeping as I crept into the hallway, Anna at my side.

They had no idea that their classmates-turned-culprits were about to commit mild sacrilege.

Anna tapped my shoulder and whispered, "It's time."

We tiptoed down the narrow hallway, avoiding the creaky floorboards we had memorized a week ago.

Barefoot, we moved silently across the cold tile floor, shoes in hand.

The only sound was our muffled laughter and the distant chiming of the bell tower striking midnight.

The laundry room door was shockingly easy to open.

Inside, the air smelled of starch and soap.

On the wall, rows of freshly pressed habits hung neatly on dowels— the uniforms of power.

Anna turned to me, wide-eyed and grinning. "Pick your poison," she whispered.

I grabbed one. The fabric was heavier than I expected. We struggled to put them on, stifling giggles as we tried to mimic the stern appearance of the sisters.

"How do they breathe in these things?" I whispered.

Anna adjusted the headpiece on me, laughing. "You look like a nun on the run."

"And you look like you're about to get us expelled."

She winked. "Only if we get caught."

The Grotto

The grotto sat at the far edge of the campus, a small stone alcove surrounded by tall hedges. In the center stood a statue of the Virgin Mary, her face serene and pale in the moonlight.

The moon hung low, casting silver light across the courtyard. It was cold, but the adrenaline kept us warm.

We ran, habits billowing behind us like wings.

"Sister Anna, slow down!" I gasped, pretending to scold her in my best nun-voice. "The Lord frowns upon such... frolicking!"

Anna doubled over laughing, nearly tripping over the long hem of the habit. "Oh, Sister, I fear I have strayed from the path!"

We ran in circles, laughing too loud, twirling like fools in the moonlight. For a moment, I forgot the suffocating rules. I forgot the weight of my father's absence. I forgot the silence.

It was just us—two girls defying the stillness of St. Agnes, claiming a sliver of freedom in a place built on obedience.

And then—"Ahem."

The sound cut through the night like a knife.

We froze.

There, standing at the edge of the grotto, illuminated by the soft glow of the chapel's stained-glass windows, was Sister Amelia Ann herself.

Her arms were crossed. Her face, a storm brewing.

Behind her, Sister Theresa, her lips pressed so tightly together it looked painful.

Anna whispered, "Well... we're dead."

I swallowed hard, my heart dropping to my knees. "Worse. We're going to hell."

The Walk of Shame

The walk back to the main building felt like a funeral march.

We still wore the habits—our evidence of sin—too afraid to remove them under the Sisters' watchful eyes.

Sister Amelia Ann didn't speak until we reached her office. The room was cold, filled with dusty books and a single crucifix hanging on the wall.

"Explain." Her voice was soft. Dangerous.

Anna, ever bold, spoke first. "We... we were honoring the sisters. By, um, trying to walk in their shoes?"

I stared at her. Really? That was her excuse?

Sister Amelia Ann arched a brow. "Honoring the sisters? By running in our sacred garments around the holy grotto—laughing?"

Anna gave a sheepish grin. "Well... when you put it like that..."

I knew we were doomed. Expelled for sure.

But then, something impossible happened.

Sister Amelia Ann sighed. Long and slow.

And for a split second—barely there—she smiled.

"Return the habits," she said at last. "Detention for the rest of the week along with cleaning floors this weekend. And consider yourselves lucky I am merciful."

As we walked back to the dorm—free, somehow unexpelled—Anna nudged me.

"Hey," she whispered. "Totally worth it."

I glanced back at the grotto in the distance. The moonlight still shimmered on the statue's face.

The night felt lighter somehow.

I laughed.

"Yeah," I whispered. "Totally worth it."

Not just for the laugh.

But for the reminder that I was still alive—and still me.

The next morning, Sister Amelia Ann handed me the phone and told me I would be the one to call my mother. I had to explain why I was staying at school for the weekend—to let her know what I had done. My voice was quiet, my heart thudding in my chest, but I told her the truth.

Sister Amelia Ann stood nearby, arms folded, listening.

It was humiliating. And a little terrifying.

But part of me understood—this was my consequence to carry.

Chapter 8
Powdered Justice

L ife at St. Agnes Academy was built on discipline, silence, and endless
rules.

But by then, I had already stopped trying to disappear.

My grief hadn't gone away—but now, it had an edge. And a sense of
humor.

The halls were cold, the wooden dormitory floors echoed with every
step, and the presence of the nuns was inescapable. Even the air felt heavy,
thick with the scent of candle wax, aged wood, and something faintly
medicinal—as if the past itself had soaked into the walls.

We were expected to be proper, obedient, and above all—silent.

But what they didn't expect?

That we'd find our own ways to survive it.

And sometimes, survival meant a little rebellion.

The Tattletale Problem

My roommate had a ritual.

Her bed had to be perfectly made. Her books lined up just right. Her
talcum powder? Sacred. The floral scent clung to everything she touched.

But for all her poise and orderliness, she had one fatal flaw.

She was a tattletale.

And not just your run-of-the-mill rule-follower—She lived to report on people.

If someone whispered after lights out—she ran to tell the nuns.

If someone rolled their skirt waistband to shorten their uniform—she made sure they got caught.

If someone passed notes in class—she turned them in without a second thought.

She had a gift for making herself invisible when she needed to eavesdrop, then reappearing just in time to drop a name to Sister Mary Martin.

And for the rest of us who lived at St. Agnes full-time, she was a thorn in our side.

Enough Was Enough

One evening, after she turned in two girls for absolutely nothing, I'd had enough.

It wasn't just her snitching—it was the smug self-righteousness she carried when she did it.

That night, while the other girls went to dinner, I stayed behind.

I had a plan.

A brilliant plan.

The Setup: A Perfectly Executed Prank

Step one: Short-sheet her bed.

I folded the bottom sheet up and over itself, so that when she climbed in, her feet would get stuck halfway down.

Step two: The talcum powder.

I lifted her blanket, carefully sprinkled a light dusting across the sheets—then decided to go big.

I dumped the entire container underneath the covers.

A cloud of white rose up, the floral scent intensifying, filling the air like a storm brewing.

I shook the blankets slightly, making sure it blended in, invisible to the eye but waiting for impact.

Step three: Put everything back perfectly.

- The blankets? Fluffed.
- The pillows? Arranged exactly how she left them.
- The talcum powder? Completely undetectable.

Then, I waited.

Sweet, Powdery Justice

That night, she went through her usual bedtime routine:
- Fifty brushstrokes to her hair.
- A perfectly folded blanket on the end of the bed.
- Her books aligned just right.

Then—the moment of truth.

She climbed into bed.

And the instant she slid her legs forward—

She hit the short-sheet.

There was a pause.

A confused grunt.

And then—

A puff of talcum powder exploded into the air.

It coated her arms, her nightgown, her perfectly organized world.

The room filled with coughing, sputtering, and a high-pitched squeal of horror.

And I—I was shaking with silent laughter, my face buried in my pillow to keep from making a sound.

The harder I tried to hold it in, the worse it got.

I was crying from it.

I had never been so proud of myself.

The Aftermath

The next morning, she stormed off to complain to Sister Amelia Ann.

I braced myself.

But then—something unexpected happened.

Sister barely reacted.

There was no detention, no lecture, no extra scrubbing duty.

Because, for the first time, the nuns weren't entirely on her side.

Maybe they had grown just as tired of her tattling as we had.

Maybe, just maybe, they secretly enjoyed the fact that someone finally got her back.

Either way—I walked out of that confrontation completely unscathed.

Or so I thought.

That afternoon, Sister Amelia Ann called me aside, her expression unreadable.

"You'll be moving into the main dormitory today," she said simply.

The main dormitory.

The one that housed fourteen other girls.

I blinked.

That hadn't been part of the plan.

"Why?" I asked, though I already knew.

"It's time for a change," she said with a small smile, as if she wasn't about to turn my entire world upside down.

By sunset, I was standing in the large, chaotic dormitory, staring at the endless row of beds, the thin, clay-colored curtains barely offering any privacy.

Gone was the semi-private space I had once had.

Gone was my little corner of quiet.

Gone was my balcony.

And in its place?

• Noise.

• Laughter.

• A whole new kind of survival.

I hadn't expected that prank to change my life.

But in the end—It had.

And I wouldn't have changed a thing.

The Price of Revenge

I knew there would be consequences.

And they came swiftly.

That afternoon, Sister Amelia Ann led me into her office and pointed to the phone.

"You'll need to call your mother," she said, her voice measured.

So I did—under her watchful eye, again. I held the receiver to my ear, explained what I had done, and that I wouldn't be coming home with my sister Alice that weekend. My mother didn't scold me.

She didn't have to. The quiet disappointment I heard in her voice settled over me heavier than any punishment.

And still, Sister Amelia Ann stood nearby, her arms folded, making sure I followed through.

Instead of going home with Alice for the weekend like I had planned, I was sentenced to stay behind at St. Agnes—a fate worse than I had imagined.

The punishment?

Scrubbing floors. Mopping hallways. Dusting the same Venetian blinds Sister Amelia Ann always assigned when she wanted to make a point.

Every time I dipped the mop into the bucket, wrung out the filthy water, and pushed it across the cold tiles, I reminded myself:

It was worth it.

Every single second.

I pictured her face again—the shock, the powder explosion, the way she had sputtered as the white cloud filled the air.

I smirked to myself, wiping sweat from my brow as I moved to the next set of blinds.

I had no regrets.

And I wouldn't have changed a thing.

Because sometimes, laughter was the only protest I had.

And in a place built on silence, a single burst of joy felt like a revolution.

Chapter 9
The Mystery in
the Alcove

The dormitory was nothing like my semi-private room.
It was chaos.

Fifteen girls. Fifteen beds. Fifteen different conversations happening at once.

And the only bed left? It was right next to Anna's. I hadn't expected that. How cool was that.

Each bed was separated only by a thin piece of fabric, meant to give us some illusion of personal space—but it did nothing to block out the constant hum of chatter, giggles, and rustling sheets.

The room smelled faintly of shampoo, teenage sweat, and the sharp tang of disinfectant that clung to the tile floors.

At night, the room came alive with whispers.

"Did you hear Sister Mary Martin today in Spanish class? She actually smiled."

"Not possible."

"I swear! Someone made a joke about Saint Francis, and she almost laughed."

Gasps. More giggles.

It was always like this—the moment the lights went out, the real conversations began. The darkness felt soft, like a blanket over our chaos, emboldening our whispers.

And then—without fail—just as we reached the peak of our laughter, a shadow would appear in the doorway.

"Quiet."

The deep, stern voice of Sister Amelia Ann rang through the room, making every girl freeze.

For a split second, there was absolute silence.

Then—one girl would let out a muffled giggle.

Then another.

And then, all at once, we were laughing again—harder this time, trying (and failing) to bury the sound in our pillows.

Sister Amelia Ann would sigh heavily, her presence lingering in the doorway. Eventually, she'd give up, muttering, "Hopeless," before disappearing down the hallway.

And that's when Anna and I got our idea.

The Mystery of the Habit

It started as a joke.

One night, as the laughter died down, Anna leaned over to my bed, her voice barely above a whisper.

"Have you ever seen a nun without her habit?"

I blinked at her. "What?"

"I mean, what do they wear to bed?" she continued, her voice filled with pure mischief. "Do they sleep in full habits? Or do they have normal pajamas? What do you think?"

I stifled a giggle. "Maybe they have long nightgowns. Maybe they shave their heads."

Anna gasped. "What if they have short hair? Or—really long hair?!"

We both dissolved into silent laughter, covering our mouths with our blankets.

And then—the idea formed.

"We have to find out," Anna whispered.

I grinned. "We're going to spy on Sister Amelia Ann."

The Alcove Mission

At the back of the dormitory, tucked into a far corner beyond the rows of beds, was a small walled-off space—an alcove. It had partial walls that didn't reach the ceiling and a curtain across the opening. Sister Amelia Ann sometimes slept there, but not every night.

Tonight, she was there.

And that meant we had one chance to solve the mystery.

Our plan? Simple.

We just needed to peek over the wall and see what she was wearing.

One problem.

The wall was too tall.

Anna and I stood beneath it, barefoot on the cold tile, shifting from foot to foot. The air felt still and heavy, like the room was holding its breath with us.

"Okay," I whispered. "I'll climb on your back, and then I'll—"

"Wait, what?" Anna hissed. "Why am I the one getting stepped on?"

I rolled my eyes. "Because I'm lighter."

She sighed dramatically. "Fine. But if you fall and kill us both, I'm blaming you."

She crouched down, bracing herself.

I carefully placed one foot onto her back.

Then the other.

I reached up, gripping the edge of the wall.

"Almost... there..."

I stretched, trying to hoist myself up just a little higher.

But then—Anna shifted.

Her arms wobbled beneath me.

My foot slipped.

And before I could stop it—

I crashed to the floor.

Loudly.

Painfully.

Right on my back.

For a moment, we both just lay there, frozen, listening.

The dormitory had gone dead silent.

You could hear the hum of the overhead light.

Someone's bed creaked.

A cough.

Then silence.

Then—click. Click.

Sister Amelia Ann's shoes.

Caught in the Act

She didn't yell.

She didn't move.

She just stood there, arms folded, staring down at us with a face carved from stone.

Anna broke first.

"...Sister," she said, her voice far too innocent. "We were just—"

Sister Amelia Ann held up a hand.

"Don't."

Anna's mouth snapped shut.

Sister Amelia Ann's eyes drifted toward the alcove wall.

Then back to us.

She exhaled slowly.

"What," she said very calmly, "were you doing?"

I opened my mouth. Nothing came out.

My heart thudded in my ears. I was sure we were about to get kicked out, reported, sent home.

But where would that even be?

James was home now—recovering.

But I still had to finish out the year at St. Agnes.

I didn't belong there anymore... but I didn't belong anywhere else either.

I didn't have a home to go back to—not really.

Just a silence no one talked about and a sadness that hung in every corner.

Maybe that's why we did it.

Why we reached for mischief like it was medicine.

"Well, we were... um... practicing teamwork?"

I gave her a look that screamed, Are you serious?

Sister Amelia Ann blinked.

Then, after a long pause, she shook her head and muttered, "I don't want to know."

We weren't expelled.

But we did get detention.

For a week.

Anna groaned when we got back to our beds. "All that, and we still don't know what she wears to bed."

I sighed. "Totally not worth it."

Anna smirked. "Yes, it was."

We grinned at each other, the silence of the dormitory once again filling with barely contained laughter.

Because even in a place like St. Agnes—where grief hung in the air and the rules felt endless—we needed something to chase.

Something to wonder about.

Something to make us feel like girls again.

Chapter 10
Friday Nights and Wool Blankets

Not everything at St. Agnes Academy was about rules, prayers, and punishment.

Sure, the nuns tried their best to keep us in line—morning chapel, stiff uniforms, silent meals.

But no amount of discipline could stop a bunch of teenage girls from finding a little fun.

Especially on Dating Game nights.

It became our tradition—one of the few times we all came together without whispered gossip or worried glances over our shoulders.

All week, we looked forward to Friday nights.

Some of the girls smuggled snacks from the dining hall. Others scouted out the best spots on the floor before the show even started.

The Dating Game was our escape.

And it all started with an old TV and a blanket.

The Setup

The TV was ancient—one of those heavy box sets with dials instead of buttons, its screen humming faintly with static when it warmed up.

The blanket we used to cover it was scratchy and smelled faintly of chapel incense and old wool—like it had once lived in a donation bin.

It sat in a cramped recreation room that smelled vaguely of chalk, pine cleaner, and years of secrets.

The nuns allowed us to watch exactly one hour of television on Friday nights.

But the best part?

They never stayed to supervise.

So, The Dating Game became our show.

"Okay, everyone! Curtain time!" Anna would declare, draping the blanket over the screen so none of us could see the contestants.

"Remember the rules," I'd add, standing beside her like her trusty assistant. "No peeking. No cheating. You can only pick based on the questions and answers."

"And your gut instinct for love!" Anna would joke, fluttering her hands dramatically.

We'd howl with laughter every time.

The Game

The room would fill with girls—some perched on the edge of chairs, others sprawled on the floor, elbows propped up on pillows.

The blanket draped over the TV gave the whole thing an air of mystery, like we were casting some grand spell.

We'd listen carefully as the bachelorette asked her questions:

"Bachelor Number One, if you were an ice cream flavor, what would you be and why?"

The voice of Bachelor Number One would come through—cool, confident, sometimes goofy.

"Bachelor Number Two, what's your idea of a perfect date?"

We'd giggle at his answer, already whispering guesses to each other.

"Bachelor Number Three, if you could take me anywhere in the world, where would we go?"

Sometimes, his answer would be swoon-worthy.

Sometimes, it was so ridiculous we couldn't breathe for laughing.

"Ooooh, definitely Bachelor Three!" Anna would swoon dramatically.

"Ugh, no way! He sounds full of himself!" I'd argue.

The whole room would erupt.

"Number One sounds sweet!"

"Number Two for sure—he's funny!"

"Three's the one! Did you hear that answer?"

And then—the big reveal.

Anna would yank the blanket off the TV with a flourish, like a magician pulling a rabbit from a hat.

"Ta-da!"

And the room would explode.

Screams. Laughter.

"NOOOO! I PICKED HIM?!" someone would wail, clutching their head in mock horror.

"That's what you get for trusting a guy who likes picnics," I'd tease.

Sometimes the one we picked was handsome, with a nice smile.

But sometimes—oh, sometimes—he was nothing like we expected.

A bad haircut.

Mismatched clothes.

The kind of face that made us burst out laughing, falling over each other, wiping tears from our eyes.

"You mean that guy was Bachelor Number Three?!"

"I proposed to that guy!"

"I need to rethink my whole life!"

Anna would be on the floor, gasping for air.

We would howl and howl until our sides hurt.

Time for Ourselves

All week we were expected to fold ourselves into the rules.

To sit straight, stay quiet, be good.

But Friday night was ours.

We needed it more than we ever let on.

Between homesickness and rules, between the ache of what we didn't say and the things we missed back home—The Dating Game was the one hour we didn't have to pretend.

We could just be girls.

For that one hour every Friday night, St. Agnes wasn't so bad.

There were no nuns frowning at us for talking too loud.

No silent prayers. No stiff rules.

Just us—laughing, shouting, and sharing inside jokes that no one else would understand.

Even Claire Donnelly, the resident tattletale, would loosen up during Dating Game nights.

"Number Two's the only one with any sense," she'd say, flipping her hair like a judge at a beauty pageant.

And no one cared about her usual snitchy attitude—not on Dating Game night.

It wasn't just about picking the best bachelor.

It was about the laughter.

The freedom.

The feeling of being together.

Because at a place like St. Agnes, where the days could feel long and lonely, those small moments of joy mattered.

They reminded us that we were still girls—Girls who could laugh until we cried.

Girls who dreamed about romance and adventure.

Girls who knew how to make any place—even an all-girls Catholic boarding school—feel like home.

Same Time Next Week?

When the show ended, we'd sit in the afterglow of our laughter.

The room would settle.

Anna would glance at me, grinning.

"Same time next week?"

"Wouldn't miss it."

And as the lights dimmed and we trudged back to our dormitories, the echoes of our laughter would follow us.

The nuns probably thought prayers and discipline were what kept us whole.

But really—It was the girls.

The laughter.

And a silly dating show behind a blanket.

Because sometimes, joy doesn't need a reason.

Sometimes, joy is choosing Bachelor Number Three and laughing until your stomach hurts when he turns out to be nothing like you imagined.

Because at a place like St. Agnes, joy wasn't just a luxury—it was survival.

And sometimes, it's the silliest things that keep you alive—laughter, friends, and the blind hope that Bachelor Number Three might be the one.

Chapter 11

63 Days to Freedom

I walked the long outer path that curved behind the school, hands tucked in the sleeves of my sweater, the cold of early spring still clinging to the air. The wind was soft but sharp, and the gravel crunched beneath my shoes with each step. Daffodils were just beginning to bloom along the walkway, their yellow petals stretching upward like tiny declarations of hope.

Sixty-three days.

That's how many I had left.

Sixty-three more mornings beneath the nuns' watchful eyes.

Sixty-three more nights listening to someone cry into her pillow—quiet sobs meant for no one, but impossible to ignore.

Sixty-three more days before I would finally be back home—back with my family, my friends, my world.

I paused at the curve, turning to face the massive building I had called home for the past seven months. It loomed against the gray sky—equal parts fortress and cathedral. The structure was perfectly symmetrical: one side housing the dormitories and classrooms, the other side closed off entirely. That was the nuns' wing.

I had never seen anyone enter or exit through their doors.

They always remained shut.

There was a finality to them—a quiet message: This part isn't for you.

The grand foyer sat in the middle, like a silent spine connecting two separate lives.

To the right, just beyond the main structure, stood the nursing home—a separate house altogether. I had volunteered there during the second half of the year. They called it "candy striping." It wasn't glamorous, but it gave me something to do. It broke up the sameness of the days and made me feel useful in a way that St. Agnes rarely did.

Inside those walls, life moved slower. Quieter. I listened to old stories, held frail hands, walked careful hallways filled with the scent of antiseptic and the rustle of soft voices behind closed doors. It was a different kind of silence. Not cold. Just still.

Now, with daffodils blooming and spring creeping in, everything felt like it was slowly waking up—including me.

Fifteen Beds, Fifteen Stories

Our dormitory sat on the second floor, packed with freshmen and sophomores. The third floor belonged to the upperclassmen—and we were never allowed up there. The staircase leading to it was strictly off-limits—one of those unspoken rules you didn't dare question.

Whatever happened up there stayed up there.

We heard rumors, of course. Supposedly, they had their own recreation room with a TV, just like us. But beyond that, the third floor remained a mystery.

We didn't mix with them.

And they made sure they didn't mix with us.

There were fifteen beds in our dormitory.

But there were more than fifteen stories behind those sheets and blankets.

Some girls moved like shadows. Others tried to take up space in a place where girls were taught to be small.

Some had always known they'd end up here—girls from wealthy families, sent away for being too rebellious, too wild, too much trouble for high society. Others had been expelled from public schools, with nowhere else to go.

And then there were girls like me.

Girls who had lived at home until life changed in an instant—until one day, we didn't.

We hadn't chosen St. Agnes.

We were here because there was nowhere else to be.

Unlike the girls who rode the bus back to their homes each afternoon, we lived here.

The day students had families waiting for them, local lives they could return to.

But the rest of us came from far away—different cities, different states, different circumstances that made weekend visits impossible.

St. Agnes wasn't just our school.

It was our world—whether we wanted it to be or not.

Some girls were counting down the days like I was.

But others?

There was no one waiting for them on the other side.

The Bus Boys of St. Michael's

Every afternoon, just before dismissal, the bus would arrive for the girls who lived nearby.

And on that bus?

Boys.

Not just any boys—St. Michael's boys.

The all-boys Catholic school was four miles down the road. And while the priests there probably tried their best to keep them in line, we all knew one thing:

They were just as wild as we were.

We leaned out the windows, forearms resting on chipped paint and dust, the wind catching the edge of our sleeves as we shouted into the afternoon light.

"Ohhh, here they come," Anna would whisper dramatically, as if we were scientists observing a rare species in the wild.

And then, the games began.

"HELLO, ST. MICHAEL'S!" I'd shout, leading the charge.

A few of the boys would glance up, grinning.

We waved, giggled, blew kisses—and once, just once, I yelled, "Marry me!" to an unsuspecting sophomore.

He grinned and shouted back, "Only if you take me away from here!"

One afternoon, Sister Amelia Ann caught us and assigned us dormitory window-scrubbing duty as punishment.

Which was fine by us—because we had a perfect view of the boys while we worked.

Anna called it a win-win. I agreed.

One Last Act of Rebellion: The Great Belching Contest of St. Agnes

With only a few weeks left before freedom, Anna and I planned one final act of rebellion.

This time it was my idea.

"You know," I said, lounging on my bed, "boredom is the devil's playground."

Anna grinned. "And what exactly does the devil do at a Catholic school with weeks left to serve?"

I held up two cans of root beer. "Belching contest."

"Oh, you're on," she said, grabbing a can.

"Loudest belch wins. Loser owes dessert for a week."

"Deal."

The first belch was modest—a warm-up.

But soon, thunderous echoes were bouncing off the walls, each belch louder than the last.

"BUUUUUURP!"

"That was weak!" I laughed. "Let me show you how it's done."

We kept going, rattling the dormitory with laughter and noise, until—

"AHEM."

We froze.

There, standing in the doorway, was Sister Mary Martin. And just behind her—Sister Amelia Ann.

Anna and I exchanged wide-eyed looks.

I whispered, "Totally worth it."

She whispered back, "Absolutely."

Where This Leaves Me

I had less than a month left.

I had a home to go back to.

I had a world outside these walls waiting for me.

The Only One Not Coming Back

The year was ending.

Suitcases were being packed. Beds stripped. Uniforms folded.

Everyone else would return in the fall.

I was going home.

I was the only one not coming back for sophomore year.

A Goodbye Between Friends

The night before I left, Anna and I sat on the edge of her bed, pretending the goodbye wasn't coming.

"You better write me," she said, her voice wavering just a little.

"I will," I promised. "And you better write me back."

We hugged—tight, longer than necessary.

In nine months, she had gone from stranger to something like family.

I didn't know what life would look like on the outside, but I knew I'd carry her with me.

A Last Look Back

Nine months.

Nine months of midnight whispers and stolen laughter.

Nine months of chapel bells marking time, of rules bent but never quite broken.

Nine months of trying to fit into a place I never chose.

Nine months of missing my dad. Missing my family.

I had arrived with a suitcase in hand, climbing those steps feeling untethered and lost.

Now, I stood at the top again—suitcase beside me—ready to leave.

But I wasn't the same girl anymore.

I took one final look at the grand, looming building—its towering windows, the long hallways that had once felt so foreign.

I had learned to navigate them, just as I had learned to navigate life without my father.

The ache of his absence hadn't faded. But it had softened—wrapped in a quiet understanding that grief and love could exist side by side.

Through all the rules, the antique furniture, the silent nights staring at the ceiling—one thing had been constant: Anna.

She had turned obligation into memories.

She had turned this place into something more.

And she was a part of me now.

The car idled at the curb, exhaust curling into the cool morning air.

My mother sat behind the wheel, smiling—a real, open smile I hadn't seen in a long time.

My brother was home now.

We were going home.

But Dad wouldn't be there.

The thought settled in my chest—heavy, yet familiar.

For a fleeting second, I imagined him standing in the doorway, arms crossed, that easy smile waiting for me.

I let myself see it. Let myself believe it.

Then I blinked—and it was gone.

I exhaled slowly, grabbed my suitcase, and ran my fingers along the cold railing beside me—one last moment.

Then I lifted the suitcase and walked down the steps.

I closed the car door behind me.

But the girl who had arrived wasn't the same one who was leaving.

I was going home.

Chapter 12
Sneakers Under the Crown

Coming home after St. Agnes felt like waking up from a long, strange dream.

Everything looked the same—our neighborhood, my high school, the curve of the driveway—but I had changed. I walked through familiar spaces with unfamiliar quiet inside me. I had learned how to survive alone. Now I had to learn how to belong again.

At first, it was awkward. I wasn't used to so much noise. So much freedom. But slowly, something began to loosen in me.

I reconnected with old friends, joined the ski club, and by junior year, I had even been nominated as a prom princess.

It didn't feel effortless. I was still learning how to be with people again. But little by little, the edges of isolation began to soften.

Ski club was my first real taste of freedom. As I flew down the slopes, the cold, crisp air hit my face and peeled away everything heavy. The icy wind helped me ignore how frozen my fingertips felt inside my gloves. I didn't care. I felt alive again. Confident. Like I had stepped outside of all the things I couldn't say.

At home, it was just me and Mom now.

And we had found our rhythm—sort of.

We'd peel apples at the kitchen counter together, prepping for her homemade applesauce. She'd drop the slices into the bowl, and I'd steal them out just as fast, eating them raw and grinning as she swatted my hand with a wooden spoon. "Those are for the pot," she'd scold, half-laughing. It was one of our small rituals—an ordinary kind of closeness that felt like peace.

There were other moments, too—like the red Mustang. I'd beg to borrow it with my most charming smile, and she'd make me promise to bring back a root beer float from the A&W. It became our deal: a little freedom for a little sugar.

She was healing in her own way. She took up ceramics, filling the house with the scent of glaze and kiln paint. She joined a network marketing company called Shaklee, built a team, started earning bonuses. She was working toward a brand-new car.

I was proud of her. After everything she had been through, she was rebuilding her life—piece by piece.

And somehow, so was I.

By then, I was dating a boy who was two years older than me. He had just graduated and gone off to broadcasting school in San Francisco. We talked on the phone, but the distance slowly faded our connection. There was no breakup—just space. A quiet drift.

A slow fade between two young hearts doing their best to grow up.

But before the summer pulled us in different directions, something unexpected happened—something I would carry with me for years.

That spring, I was chosen as the Junior May Day Princess. I'll never forget the night of the dress rehearsal. We were in the high school gymnasium, the lights dimmed, the bleachers filled with scattered parents and faculty.

After I stepped forward, did my curtsy, and the spotlight moved on, I caught a glimpse of my mom sitting in the crowd. She was beaming. Her face glowed with pride in a way I hadn't seen since before my father died.

In that moment, I felt something settle in my chest—a shared happiness, something we had both earned.

But under my dress that night, I was wearing sneakers. White canvas ones with a red peace sign inked on the sides. I had drawn it myself—part rebellion, part signature. When I curtsied during rehearsal, I lifted the hem just a little higher than necessary, just enough to catch the light. Mom had no idea, but I grinned to myself the whole way home.

The real night was different.

No sneakers.

Just my princess dress—soft blue, simple but elegant—and the delicate tiara they placed on my head as part of the tradition. I had an escort, a classmate in a suit too big for him, and together we walked out beneath the gymnasium lights while the announcer read my name.

I don't remember what song was playing.

I remember my dress brushing the tops of my heels.

I remember smiling without trying.

I remember my mom's face in the crowd, glowing.

That night, when it was over, I drove home in her candy-apple-red Mustang, windows down, music up, tiara still pinned into my curls. She teased me like always—"Hope you brought back my root beer float"—and I did.

It felt like something had been mended.

Not everything.

But something.

By then, I was borrowing her candy-apple-red Mustang and driving it through town like it was made of magic. She'd tease me, saying, "You can use the car—but only if you bring me back a root beer float from A&W."

It became our standing deal. A little freedom traded for a little sweetness.

But it wasn't perfect. Not even close.

Because grief is messy, and healing is never a straight line.

There was still anger under the surface—especially toward her. I never told her how abandoned I'd felt that year at St. Agnes. How angry I was for being sent away during the most painful season of my life.

Instead of talking about it, I wrote it down. Poured it onto paper in a moment of frustration.

I called her a name I can barely admit now.

I wrote it in a note, to Leah, my best friend, thinking it would never be seen.

One word—just one—but it carried every ounce of pain I hadn't figured out how to speak.

I called her a bitch.

And then she found it.

I was at church camp on the coast when she called. Her voice was quiet, cold. She told me she wouldn't be picking me up. Not this time. Not after that.

So it was Leah and her mom who drove the two hours to get me.

I was too stunned. Too ashamed. But underneath the embarrassment, I knew what it was really about. I was still hurting. Still furious. Still fourteen inside, standing in the hallway at St. Agnes, begging her not to leave.

That rift between us didn't last forever. We didn't talk about the note again. We didn't talk about that year much at all. But little by little, we kept showing up for each other. Through applesauce and A&W floats. Through laughter and silence.

We were healing, she and I.

Not all at once. Not perfectly.

But healing.

And for a little while, we weren't just surviving—we were almost living again.

Chapter 13

The Room
Without Air

My senior year started like any other.

Friends talked about who they were dating, the next football game, where we planned to go after graduation. We were living in the moment, soaking up every second, convinced that life was nothing but wide-open possibilities.

The Vietnam War still cast its shadow, and opinions about it buzzed through the hallways. One of my classmates even took the school board to court—and won the right to wear his hair long. A quiet kind of rebellion, but it meant something.

The world was changing.

And so were we.

We spent our lunch periods huddled around cafeteria tables, trading music recommendations, talking about part-time jobs and the next dance. It was the '70s—long hair, bell-bottoms, and music that promised freedom, defiance, and dreams bigger than our small town.

Life felt electric.

The future felt limitless.

The Invitation

Leah—my best friend—told me her brother was home from college, and he and his friends were throwing a party.

Music, lights, laughter.

The pulse of the night pulling me forward.

Strobe lights would be flashing.

The Bee Gees would be playing.

The rhythm of the era—irresistible and alive—called to me.

I wanted to go.

More than that—I needed to.

But Mom?

She didn't want me to.

She said it softly but firmly.

"Please don't go," she said, her eyes holding mine a little longer than usual.

Maybe it was worry.

Maybe it was something deeper.

But I brushed it off.

Told her I'd be fine.

And then I went.

The Party

It was everything I expected.

Music thumped through the house, strobe lights slicing through the dark.

The Bee Gees played in the background.

Everywhere, people were laughing, dancing, alive.

It felt carefree.

It felt like the world was opening its arms—Exactly the kind of night senior year deserved.

As the hours passed, people drifted away.

The lights dimmed.

The music faded.

The party wound down.

Like always, I planned to share a bed with Leah.

We'd done that countless times—talking and laughing until sleep claimed us.

I always teased her about her polyester nightgowns.

"These things are so slimy," I'd say.

"Seriously, how do you even sleep in this?"

She'd laugh and toss a pillow at me.

It was familiar.

Safe.

But that night felt different.

Something Felt Off

I lay beside her for a while, trying to settle.

But I couldn't.

Something felt off.

Restless, I got up and stepped into the darkened living room.

The house was quiet now.

Everyone had gone.

I found a couch and lay down, hoping sleep would come.

The silence pressed against the windows.

A streetlight buzzed beyond the curtains.

I closed my eyes.

I drifted.

The Moment Everything Changed

And then—It happened.
At first, I thought I was dreaming.
That blurry space between sleep and waking.
But this wasn't a dream.
The air shifted.
A shadow moved.
I felt the couch dip beside me.
Before my mind could catch up—Pressure.
A body.
Heavy.
Pinning me down.
The weight crushed the breath from my lungs.
I gasped.
But no sound came out.
The room, once so familiar, turned foreign.
Cold.
This isn't happening.
But it was.

Trapped

I tried to move.
But the weight bore down harder.
Panic roared through me, wild and useless.
My mind screamed Move!—but my body wouldn't listen.
Everything was happening too fast.
No time to think.
No space to understand.

Silenced
Stop.
Please stop.
But the words never came.
The smell of beer.
Of sweat.
The suffocating closeness.
I couldn't push it away.
I was smothered.
Crushed beneath something I couldn't fight.
And then—As suddenly as it began—It ended.

Frozen in Time

The weight lifted.
The air returned.
But I didn't move.
I couldn't.
I lay there, stunned.
Small.
Broken.
The couch felt unfamiliar beneath me.
The darkness heavier than before.
I stared at the ceiling, willing my breath to steady.
What just happened?
But deep down—I already knew.

The Bathroom

I don't remember getting up.

But suddenly, I was in the bathroom.

The overhead light buzzed.

The mirror blurred.

My skin felt too tight.

My breath too shallow.

I grabbed a stack of washcloths, turned on the water, and began scrubbing.

Hard.

Frantically.

I scrubbed everywhere—even places that didn't need it.

I couldn't stop.

My hands moved with panic, with urgency, with grief I hadn't yet named.

And then I saw it.

Blood.

Small stains at first. Then more.

I froze.

I stood there, staring.

The reality sinking in like cold water.

This wasn't a dream.

Not a nightmare.

It was real.

And I knew—everything had changed.

The Night That Didn't End

I stayed there for what felt like hours.

Not sleeping.

Not crying.

Just existing.

Frozen.

The house was silent.

But inside me, everything was screaming.

Thoughts crashed and collided.

If I hadn't gone...

If I had listened to her...

But none of it mattered now.

Because the truth was simple:

Everything had changed.

A Line Drawn in Time

I would never forget the feeling of that night.

The helplessness.

The shock.

The confusion.

The loss.

It was supposed to be just a party.

But it wasn't.

It became a dividing line.

A moment that marked everything before—And everything after.

Chapter 14
The Quiet Decision

In the days that followed, I told myself it hadn't happened.

I moved through school like a ghost—silent, hollow, hoping that if I didn't speak the truth, maybe it wouldn't be real.

But there was no outrunning it.

Senior year was supposed to be full of excitement—prom dresses, graduation rehearsals, college acceptance letters.

I had imagined walking across the stage, diploma in hand, ready to take on the world.

Instead, I was watching it all slip away.

I hadn't told anyone the truth, but my body had begun to speak for me. There was no hiding it anymore. And in a town like ours, the whispers had already begun.

The college talks, the countdowns my friends whispered about between classes—I watched it all from the outside, knowing none of it was meant for me anymore.

By April, there was no denying it.

I was pregnant.

The mornings filled with sickness had turned into days filled with fear.

I had managed to hide it for a while, but eventually, the truth became something I could no longer conceal.

At home, I wore loose clothing and stayed in my room after school, avoiding conversations.

Avoiding eyes.

Avoiding reality.

The Conversation

My sister closest in age became my only confidante.

She knew people—people who had gone to Mexico, to underground clinics.

"No one would have to know," she said. "You could just... move on."

The words hung between us—weightless and impossible all at once.

But for me, it wasn't simple.

It could never be.

It was the early 1970s, and though no one spoke openly about sexual violence, they did talk about this.

Quietly.

Carefully.

In hushed voices behind closed doors.

To some, it was a decision—a way to reclaim a future that had been derailed.

To me, it was something else entirely.

The Quiet Decision

I sat with those conversations.

I turned them over and over in my mind during long, sleepless nights, staring up at the ceiling.

I could have made it all disappear.

No one would ever know.

Life could go back to how it was—at least on the outside.

And sometimes, when the ache crept in late at night, I wondered—what if I had listened to my mother? What if I hadn't gone to the party?

One night, lying alone in the dark, I placed my hand over my stomach.

Felt the slightest curve.

The faintest rise.

The smallest, most fragile life.

My life had already been rewritten in ways I hadn't chosen.

But this life—this tiny, silent life—was mine to protect.

And in that moment, fear gave way to something stronger:

Resolve.

One day, quietly and fully, I made the decision.

A decision that felt bigger than all the fear, the shame, the uncertainty.

This wasn't an option for me.

I was going to keep the new life forming within me.

I didn't know how.

I didn't know what kind of future I could offer.

But I knew I couldn't make the other choice.

This life—this new, growing life—was now part of me.

And I would not abandon it.

Leaving Home

I stayed silent.

Because I was ashamed.

Because I felt guilty, even though I hadn't done anything wrong...

So, I stayed silent.

I didn't tell my mother.

I didn't share the weight of my decision with my friends.

Because deep down, I knew they wouldn't understand.

They were still dreaming about proms and graduations, college dorms and late-night talks about the future.

But my future looked different now.

By May, the truth could no longer be hidden.

I had no plan, no answers—only the certainty that I couldn't stay.

So I made my move.

I told myself I was protecting her.

Dad had been a respected mayor. A dentist. Our name still meant something in town. I didn't want to embarrass her—not with whispers, not with gossip, not with the weight of public shame.

My young mind believed that if I left before I started showing, I could spare her the disgrace.

That I could shield what remained of our family's image.

But the truth was—I was scared.

I didn't want people staring at me.

I didn't want the questions.

I didn't want the pity.

So I left.

I left my mother a note—short, without explanation—just enough to let her know I was leaving, and that I would be safe.

I folded the paper with shaking hands, set it on the kitchen counter, and walked out the door without looking back.

I took the little bit of savings I had, bought a plane ticket, and flew to California.

Memories of California

But California wasn't unfamiliar.

My mother had put me on a plane several times during my freshman year to visit my oldest brother in the Bay Area.

Those visits had been filled with laughter and adventure—memories from a different life, a different time.

I remember those trips vividly.

My brother would meet me at the San Francisco airport, always with a grin on his face.

The first thing we'd do was ditch the clothes that screamed "high school girl"—the skirt, saddle shoes, and neat jacket I always wore.

He'd hand me a tie-dyed T-shirt, a pair of jeans, and some sandals.

And just like that, I felt transformed.

Free.

We explored the streets of San Francisco like locals.

We drove up and down Haight-Ashbury, the epicenter of the counterculture movement.

The streets buzzed with life—people wearing flowers in their hair, musicians playing on street corners, and the unmistakable scent of freedom in the air.

One trip, we went to the Fillmore West.

And there, just as she was becoming a legend, I saw Janis Joplin perform.

Her voice—raw, powerful, electric—echoed through the room.

It was like watching history happen, though we didn't realize it at the time.

We even spent a day at the lake in San Francisco, renting paddle boats and lazily drifting across the water.

The sun warmed our faces, and for a little while, life felt untouched by pain or worry.

Those were carefree days.

Days when the future felt wide open and golden.

A Different Journey

But this time, going to California was different.

I wasn't visiting for fun.

I wasn't coming with stories from home or eager for another tour of the city.

I was running.

Running from the truth I couldn't speak.

From the stares I feared.

From a future I didn't know how to face.

Before, the plane rides had felt like adventure.

A getaway from routine.

But this time, I wasn't flying toward excitement.

I was flying into the unknown.

The same city.

The same airport.

But nothing about it felt familiar anymore.

Because I wasn't the same girl anymore.

The plane ride felt different, too.

Heavier.

I stared out the window at the clouds drifting past, remembering those earlier trips—the laughter, the freedom.

But now, the weight of my decision settled deep in my chest.

I knew the road ahead wouldn't be easy.

I was carrying a life I hadn't planned for, in a world that wouldn't understand.

But I wasn't running from it.

Not anymore.

Because I had chosen.

This life was staying.

And no matter what came next,

I would face it.

Not just for myself.

But for both of us.

Chapter 15
Come Home

When I stepped off the plane, my brother and sister-in-law met me with open arms.

Their embrace was warm, steady, familiar. And for a moment, I almost believed I could outrun the truth.

In the car ride home, I told them the truth. I was pregnant.

They were stunned. My brother stared straight ahead, his knuckles tight on the wheel. My sister-in-law turned toward me, eyes wide with shock and concern. No one said anything at first. The silence was thick—full of questions, disbelief, and the weight of something too big to process all at once. But eventually, they nodded. They said they understood. And that's when the focus shifted: "You need to make a call," my brother said.

But almost immediately, the tone shifted.

"You need to make a call," my brother said, his voice firm.

"Right now."

I hesitated, my heart pounding.

"You need to tell your mother where you are," my sister-in-law added. "And you need to tell her the truth."

The truth.

That I was pregnant.

The words hung in the air, heavier than anything I had carried so far.

The Moment I Had Been Avoiding

Before I picked up that phone, all I could think about was everything we had been through—my mother and I. We had worked hard just to get back to some version of peace after my father died. Our grief came out in different ways—hers through silence and routine, mine through distance and anger. I had called her a name in a note I never meant for her to see. And she had left me at church camp, unwilling to come when I needed her.

We had hurt each other. Not on purpose. But because we were both hurting.

And now I was about to make the hardest call of my life. To tell her I was pregnant.

I wasn't ready.

That was why I had run.

I thought I could put off the hardest part.

But here it was—waiting for me.

That call.

The one thing I had been trying to outrun since the moment I packed my suitcase.

Fear, shame, and uncertainty crashed down as I stared at the phone.

It sat there on the table like a test I hadn't studied for.

The phone cord twisted around my fingers. My hands were sweating. My pulse thudded in my throat. The walls felt too quiet.

What would she say?

Would she be angry?

Would she be ashamed of me?

Would I hear it in her voice—that quiet disappointment that cuts deeper than shouting ever could?

What if this ruined everything between us?

What if I lost the only parent I had left?

I closed my eyes, took a breath that barely filled my lungs, and dialed.

The Call That Changed Everything

The phone rang once.

Twice.

And then—

"Hello?"

It was her.

My mother.

Her voice—steady, familiar, home.

I opened my mouth, but no sound came.

For a long moment, I just stood there, clutching the receiver like a lifeline I was afraid to hold onto.

But I had come too far to turn back now.

"Mom... it's me."

Silence.

And then, the words tumbled out—halting, raw.

Where I was.

Why I had left.

And the truth I had carried alone for so long.

"I'm pregnant."

I braced myself.

For the anger.

For the shame.

For the disappointment I was sure would follow.

But what I heard next stunned me.

Her voice—soft and steady:

"I know. Come home."

A lump rose in my throat.

I clutched the receiver tighter, hardly believing what I had heard.

"How did you know?" I whispered.

Another pause.

"Why else would someone leave school and home in an instant?"

Then, gently—like the answer had always been that simple:

"Come home. We'll go through this together. You're not alone."

And suddenly, I remembered being little—sick with the flu, her hand on my forehead, a cool cloth on my face. She always showed up when it counted.

For a moment, I couldn't speak.

Tears welled before I could stop them.

After all the fear, all the shame, all the running—

I wasn't alone.

That one sentence cracked something open inside me.

The weight I had carried—tucked beneath layers of guilt and secrecy—began to lift.

She knew.

And she still wanted me home.

That call changed everything.

For the first time in months, I felt the ground beneath me again.

I had made my decision—to keep this life growing inside me.

And now, I knew I wouldn't face it alone.

My mother would be there.

We would face the pregnancy.

The birth.

The future.

Together.

But "together" didn't always mean we agreed.

A Choice Already Made

When I got home, my mother asked if I'd ever consider giving the baby to my oldest sister, Alice.

It wasn't said unkindly—it was a practical suggestion in her eyes. She saw Alice as stable. Married. Settled. She thought it might be the best path forward.

Then, without telling me, she called Randy.

Randy was a boy I had met at church camp the summer after my sophomore year. We'd stayed in touch. He was tall, good-looking, kind— a year older than me. He had called and asked me to attend his senior prom with him. She and Alice had even driven me three hours away so I could attend. We'd stayed in a hotel. My mom liked him that much.

She called him when I was home, pregnant.

I don't know what she said. But not long after, Randy called me.

He said he wanted to marry me. That he would give the baby a name. A father.

I hung up the phone and just sat there, stunned.

It was the '70s. Moms thought like that then. Respectability mattered. Appearances mattered.

But I had already made my decision.

I sat there shaking my head and holding my belly. No.

And then, one day, she opened the front door, and in walked her pastor. I put my hand up to both of them without saying a word.

It was my way of saying "No."

And then I turned and walked away.

By then, the baby was kicking. A constant, gentle reminder.

This was already my baby.

And I had already chosen us.

Chapter 16
What Love
Sounds Like

I thought I understood what labor would feel like.

I had heard the stories—women who knew my mother, neighbors and friends, each with their own tale.

Some spoke of quick, barely-a-struggle deliveries.

Others described long, exhausting hours that stretched endlessly.

I had listened, nodded, believed I knew what to expect.

But at eighteen, I knew my path to motherhood would be different.

Mine wasn't the story people told with warm smiles and knowing glances.

I would be a young, unwed mother.

A single parent.

The kind of journey no one talked about.

The kind of journey I knew would be hard.

And I never fooled myself about that part.

I would no longer have anything in common with my friends.

Their lives revolved around dances, dates, and plans for college.

Their dreams sparkled with freedom and discovery.

Mine had shifted.

My world would soon revolve around someone new—someone entirely dependent on me.

The things I would come to know as a mother weren't even on their horizons.

And yet, despite the fear, the isolation, the uncertainty—I was ready.

Waiting for the Moment

As the days passed and the time drew closer, my anticipation grew.

I would cradle my round belly, feeling the gentle fluttering kicks from within.

With each movement, a mix of emotions washed over me.

Excitement. Fear. Anxiousness.

Would the baby be a boy or a girl?

Would they have my eyes? My smile?

Would they look anything like me at all?

I thought about it constantly.

My family gave me a small baby shower—simple but thoughtful.

I had everything I would need:

- Soft, neutral-colored baby clothes.
- Stacks of cloth diapers.
- A bassinet placed right beside my bed.

Each night, before I slept, I would run my fingers along the edge of that bassinet.

A quiet ritual. A reminder.

I smiled and opened each tiny outfit with care, thanking everyone for coming. But there was a quiet ache I didn't show—because beneath the wrapping paper and pastel ribbons,

I still felt like the girl who had taken a different path.

I wondered if anyone else could feel that too.

That soon, very soon, my life would change forever.

That last night, I lay awake in the quiet, one hand resting on my belly, feeling the steady rhythm of tiny movements beneath my skin.

I whispered promises into the dark—That I would protect him.

That I would love him.

That somehow, we would find our way.

I didn't know what the future would hold.

But I knew it would begin soon. Very soon.

And then—The day arrived.

Labor & Delivery

The first contractions began in the early hours of the morning.

At first, they were gentle—an hour apart—barely more than dull cramps.

Manageable.

But as the hours passed, they came faster, sharper, demanding my attention in a way nothing else ever had.

Was I ready for this?

The question echoed in my mind.

Fear gripped me.

I thought about the sleepless nights ahead, the endless feedings and diaper changes.

I thought about the stares, the whispered judgments.

Would people see me as just another teenage mother?

None would know the truth. How this life had begun.

Would I be enough for this child?

Somewhere in the blur of pain, I remembered Randy's voice on the phone—the promise of a name, a father, a life I could have chosen.

But this child didn't need someone else's name.

He already had mine.

The contractions came quicker now, each one pulling me deeper into the reality that there was no turning back.

The hospital room was a blur of white sheets, sharp antiseptic smells, and the quiet beeping of machines.

My mother's hand was the only steady thing—her thumb tracing slow circles over mine, grounding me.

Outside the window, the world kept moving, unaware that mine was about to change forever.

Twelve hours passed this way.

By late afternoon, I was exhausted.

The epidural had worn off, and the pain returned with full force.

But strangely, the pain demanded so much of my energy, my mind had no room for fear.

I focused on the rhythm of it—The rise, the peak, the slow ebb—until the next wave crashed again.

I barely noticed the moment when, in a surge of unbearable intensity, I bit down hard on my mother's hand.

She didn't pull away.

She only squeezed back, steady and reassuring.

And then—The world shifted.

The air seemed to still.

A cry pierced the room.

"It's a boy," the nurse said, and time seemed to pause.

They placed him in my arms—a tiny, warm bundle of life.

His skin smelled faintly of powder and something sweeter, something only newborns seem to carry.

His cry, though small, filled the entire room and echoed straight into my heart.

All the fear, the anxiety, the uncertainty—It fell away in that moment.

Because nothing prepares you for the joy that comes with seeing your child for the first time.

Nothing prepares you for the overwhelming love that springs to life when your eyes meet this small, perfect being who came from you.

Tears blurred my vision, and I held him close.

His tiny fingers curled instinctively around mine, a grasp so small, so fierce, it made my heart ache.

In that moment, I knew.

This was the beginning of everything.

I named him Jonathan Klady.

Jonathan, because it meant "God has given"—a gift from God.

Klady, because it was my father's middle name, a way to honor the man whose love and strength

I still carried with me.

He had been my safe place, the one person I trusted completely. Even though he was gone, I wanted Jonathan to carry that part of him forward.

Jonathan weighed six pounds, four ounces—tiny, perfect, and so incredibly precious.

He was my new beginning.

But life has a way of testing you when you least expect it.

The Surgery

Shortly after Jonathan's birth, the doctors told me he had a hernia.

Not just any hernia—one large enough to require surgery.

Surgery—on my newborn baby.

The word alone was enough to make my heart race and my mind swirl with questions.

How could this be happening?

He was so small, so new to this world.

How could his tiny body endure this?

The doctor reassured me:

- The surgery was common in newborn boys.
- It would take less than an hour.
- Jonathan wouldn't feel pain.

I tried to hold onto his words, but the fear in my heart was hard to quiet.

Jonathan was just three days old when he went in for surgery.

Three days old.

I kissed his forehead, whispering prayers that he would be okay.

The surgery took less than an hour, just as the doctor promised.

Everything had gone well.

Relief washed over me, but I still had to wait.

Jonathan would stay overnight for observation.

My arms ached to hold him, to take him home and never let him go.

That morning, I was released from the hospital, but I raced back at noon to feed him.

The staff were wonderful.

They had a warm bottle ready, knowing I would be there.

I stayed the entire day, unwilling to miss a single moment.

Watching him sleep peacefully, I felt a mixture of gratitude and protectiveness I had never known before.

My little boy had already proven he was stronger than I could have imagined.

Going Home

The next day, I could bring Jonathan home.

I fed him in the morning, then rushed home to get my mother. She would be driving us.

For the first time, the word home meant something new.

It meant the beginning of our lives together.

Jonathan Klady—my gift from God.

My father's name carried in his, a symbol of strength passed down.

A new life.

A new beginning.

And together, we would face whatever came next.

I wasn't the same girl who had feared being alone, judged, or misunderstood.

I was a mother now.

Stronger.

Braver.

And as I held Jonathan close, I realized:

I wasn't alone at all.

That night, I sat in the hospital chair, the room dim and quiet except for the soft hum of machines.

I pulled Jonathan close, his warm weight against my chest, and listened to the sound of his breathing.

I didn't know what tomorrow would bring.

But I knew one thing:

I was his mother.

And we had already begun.

Chapter 17
Life Is Fragile

It was just after noon on August 28, and the sky wore a patchwork of sunlight and lingering clouds.

The night before had brought the first rain in five weeks—a welcome relief, washing away the dust of a long, dry spell.

I had spent the entire day and night before thinking about this moment, preparing for it, waiting for it.

And now, as morning arrived, it felt like the universe had listened.

The clouds moved slowly, reluctant to let go, but the sun broke through in golden shafts that danced across the pavement.

The air smelled fresh and earthy—the scent of new beginnings.

Today, I was bringing my son home.

The Drive from the Hospital

Jonathan,

Three days old.

I had dressed him in the softest baby blue outfit, wrapping him snugly in a matching blanket.

Every hour, my attachment to him had deepened. This tiny life, so new, so vulnerable, was now part of me in a way I hadn't expected.

Mom pulled up to the hospital curb in her cherry-red 1965 Mustang. I climbed into the passenger seat, heart fluttering—not with fear, but with awe. Awe that he was here. That he was mine.

A nurse leaned in, gently placing Jonathan in my arms. I carefully secured him in the infant carrier beside me on the front seat.

And when I cradled him—truly held him close for the first time outside hospital walls—something shifted inside me.

His fingers curled into soft little fists, his rosebud lips gently pursed. His cheeks were round and pink, his tiny nose nestled into the folds of his blanket.

His skin, still wrinkled from birth, felt impossibly smooth against my fingertips.

I looked down at him and knew: this child was mine.

Not just in biology. Not just in name.

He was mine in every sacred, permanent sense of the word.

Mom and I talked softly as she drove. About dreams. About what came next. About how love could feel this immediate, this complete.

The road ahead unfurled like a ribbon beneath us, and sunlight glinted off the wet pavement.

To our right, a wide river ran parallel to the road. The water sparkled where the sun struck it, its current slow and steady, mirroring our calm.

It felt like the world had paused to celebrate this moment with us.

I should have felt safe. But something in the back of my mind—something I couldn't name—felt unsettled.

I didn't know then that everything was about to change.

The Moment Everything Changed

Jonathan was in the carrier beside me in the front seat.

He made an adorable cooing sound—one of those soft, sweet noises only a newborn can make.

Mom glanced over, her face softening for just a second.

And then—The calm shattered.

A low hum rose from beneath the tires.

At first, I barely noticed it.

Then the hum shifted—rising in pitch, gaining speed.

The sound of tires losing grip.

The road was slicker than it looked.

Mom's hands tightened on the wheel.

I turned toward her. Her eyes met mine.

Wide. Terrified.

A silent question. A silent plea.

Then—Brakes slammed.

Tires screamed.

For one fleeting moment, the world stood still.

And then—Impact.

A violent blur of motion and sound.

The Mustang spun.

The world tilted.

Light and shadow crashed into each other.

The moment stretched.

Endless. Disorienting.

And then—A final, deafening crash.

Glass rained like diamonds.

The air filled with the sharp scent of metal, rubber, and fear.

The Aftermath

I don't remember when the movement stopped.

Only the silence that followed.

The kind of silence that feels loud.

I was on the ground.

I knew I was hurt. Badly.

The skin of my cheek pressed against rocks and gravel. Pain radiated through me in sharp, stabbing bursts.

Above me, the cliff we had gone over rose like a jagged scar against the sky.

A tire spun in place.

Smoke drifted upward.

Everything else was still.

I saw the mangled car below me.

Tried to reach it.

But my body wouldn't move.

Pain held me hostage.

I cried out, but the sound never made it past my lips.

Then—I began to crawl.

Hand over hand.

Clawing through the earth.

I didn't know where the strength came from.

I needed to get help—for Jonathan. For my mother. I could see the mangled car below, but I could not reach it. I couldn't get down to them.

I could only go up. The air smelled like smoke—thick, sharp, and unnatural. It was coming from one of the tires, still spinning somewhere below.

Pain lanced through my body with every movement, but it didn't matter.

Somewhere out there—somewhere below—my son needed me.

Jonathan.

His name became my heartbeat, my breath, my only thought.

Hand over hand.

Broken nails digging into dirt and stone.

Up.

Up.

Up.

I was no longer thinking. Only moving.

Only surviving.

Life didn't wait.

It didn't pause for grief or shock.

It just shattered—and left you to pick up the pieces.

Chapter 18
Awakening

Confusion clung to me like a heavy fog.

I drifted between dreams and a reality I wasn't ready to face.

My mind waded through shadows, each breath shallow, unfamiliar.

My body remembered before my mind did.

A heaviness.

A hollow space where something vital had been.

But I couldn't name it yet.

I only knew I was broken in ways no doctor could fix.

Something cold lingered in the air.

The sharp scent of disinfectant stung my nose.

The steady hum of machines filled the silence—distant voices murmuring in hushed tones, barely audible but constant.

I tried to move.

But my body felt foreign—heavy, numb, like it no longer belonged to me.

Where am I?

The realization dawned slowly, each fragment of awareness snapping into place with painful clarity.

Hospital.

A pulse of panic surged through me.

How long had I been here?

My breath hitched.

The weight on my chest was unbearable—suffocating, relentless.

I forced my eyes open, blinking against the harsh fluorescent light filtering through the half-drawn curtains.

The world came into focus in pieces.

- Pale ceilings.
- White walls.
- A monitor beeping in slow, steady rhythm.

Everything felt cold, unfamiliar, hollow.

And then—I saw him.

Randy.

A neighbor. A close family friend. A familiar face in an unfamiliar world.

He stood by my bedside, still and silent.

What I didn't know until much later was that Randy had driven past the scene of the accident—past the flashing lights and crumpled metal—on his way home. He didn't know it was us. Not at first.

But when he heard, he rushed to the hospital.

And now, here he was. Watching over me.

His smile was faint—strained, fragile. It wasn't a smile of relief or joy. It carried a quiet sadness, filled with words he wasn't ready to say.

Our eyes met.

And in that moment, I knew.

I wasn't ready for what they held.

I didn't want to understand.

The Moment of Realization

I tried to speak.

But something was wrong.

The sound that came out was muffled, foreign, unnatural.

Panic surged again as I reached for my mouth—Braces. Bars. Wires.

My jaw was locked shut.

The shock hit like a physical blow.

I tried to speak, to ask what had happened, but my mouth was wired shut. The words came out mangled and low—barely more than a mumble.

"She's gone."

Silence fell.

The hum of machines faded into the background.

The words lingered in the air—fragile, yet final.

Randy didn't speak.

He didn't have to.

His head dipped in a slow nod—small, simple, devastating.

That nod told me everything.

The pressure in my chest deepened, a suffocating ache I couldn't escape.

My worst fear was real.

Yes.

The word echoed, bounced, settled into the hollow space inside me.

Yes.

My mother.

Gone.

A tremor rippled through me beneath the hospital sheets.

The ache in my chest wasn't just physical—It was deeper.

Raw.

A wound untouched by medicine.

The sun could have shone brightly outside, but inside, darkness reigned.

And yet, despite everything—I didn't think of Jonathan.

The morphine dulled my pain, blurred the edges of reality.

Grief drifted through me in slow, heavy waves, but it was incomplete.

The medicine softened the sharpest edges, numbing not just my body but something deeper—my awareness, my instincts.

I existed in a haze of loss, but not once did my mind reach for my son.

Not until several days later.

The Second Loss

The door opened.

I turned my head, my movements sluggish, my mind still swimming between worlds.

I was still slipping in and out of sleep.

I didn't know what day it was, or how long I'd been there.

The light in the room didn't match anything I could anchor myself to.

Time didn't move in hours or days. It moved in shadows and silence.

I was drifting through something I couldn't name.

I saw my brother's face, James, but I couldn't place the expression he wore.

James sat beside me, hesitating.

And then he said the words.

The words that shattered whatever was left of me.

"Jonathan didn't make it."

Jonathan.

The name hit me like a physical force.

The name I hadn't thought to ask for.

The world tilted.

Sound dulled, flattened.

I could see James's lips move, but for a moment, the words didn't make sense.

Then they did.

And everything inside me broke.

The room closed in.

The walls, the ceiling, the beeping of machines—everything blurred, everything collapsed inward around that single, unchangeable truth.

I had been awake.

I had been breathing.

And yet—I hadn't remembered my own son.

Terror seized me.

My mind raced, desperate to reclaim something—anything.

But there was nothing.

No memory of asking for him.

No whispered thought of his name.

Only emptiness.

The realization crushed me beneath its weight.

How could I not have thought of him?

How could I not have known?

The morphine. The shock. The pain.

It had stolen my grief.

And now, it came all at once.

The Memories That Wouldn't Let Go

Memories came unbidden, slicing through the haze.

- Jonathan's soft skin against mine.
- His tiny fingers wrapped around my thumb.
- The warmth of his body, swaddled in a pale blue blanket.

My mother's laughter—bright, full of life.

I could still hear it, still see the way her eyes crinkled when she smiled, still smell the faint trace of her perfume.

But now, all of it was gone.

I turned my face toward the window, hoping the darkness behind my eyelids would swallow me whole.

But there was no escape.

The images, the sounds—They remained.

Sharp. Unrelenting.

Trauma doesn't just take the people you love.

It steals the moments, too.

The first cries.

The whispered goodbyes.

The chance to remember them before the world goes silent.

The Final Confirmation

The silence between James and me on that day stretched endlessly.

It carried all the words that would never be spoken, all the futures that would never come to pass.

Each breath felt like a battle.

For a fleeting moment, I wished I could drift back into unconsciousness.

To forget.

To undo.

But I couldn't.

I was still here.

The mumbled words escaped before I could stop them—soft, fragile, but resolute:

"They're both gone?" I whispered for final confirmation.

The question trembled in the air, as delicate as glass.

James's nod came again—gentle, steady, final.

Yes.

A single tear slipped down my cheek.

I didn't wipe it away.

The ache in my chest tightened further, burrowing deep.

My mother.

My son.

Jonathan.

The ache wasn't temporary.

It was something I would carry always—A weight that would become part of me.

The world outside could bathe itself in sunlight.

It didn't matter.

My world had dimmed.

And yet—Somehow, I was still here.

I didn't know how to carry this kind of grief. But I knew I had to keep breathing.

Even in the dark.

Chapter 19
The Mirror

I don't know how long I lay in that hospital bed.
Time had lost its shape.

Hours bled into days, and days blurred into something unmeasurable—a quiet rhythm broken only by moments when I drifted from the haze of sleep into flashes of sharp, disorienting awareness.

There was movement around me—doctors and nurses coming and going, voices murmuring just beyond my reach.

Machines hummed and beeped in steady patterns, anchoring me to a world I barely felt part of.

One doctor stood out, a constant among the blur.

He explained that I had fractured my jaw, that I had been hurt badly. But they had managed to perform surgery, to wire my jaw back together.

He spoke gently, reassuringly—but his words felt distant, like they belonged to someone else's story.

A Numbness That Went Beyond Pain

The silence was almost louder than the machines.

It echoed in the space where thoughts should have been.

The numbness ran deep—physical, yes, but also emotional.

It wrapped itself around my chest, my mind, my memory. Like a thick, invisible blanket that protected me from a truth I wasn't yet strong enough to face.

And in some strange way, I welcomed it.

The First Time I Saw Myself

Eventually came the first day I could get out of bed on my own.

My legs felt uncertain, as if they were borrowing their strength from someone else.

I shuffled slowly toward the bathroom, gripping the doorframe for balance before stepping inside.

The bathroom was small, the air heavy with the sterile scent of disinfectant.

I gripped the sink for balance, my legs trembling.

Part of me didn't want to look.

Part of me already knew.

And there—I saw it.

The mirror.

I wasn't ready.

For a long moment, I didn't recognize the reflection staring back at me.

My head, my face—wrapped in white gauze.

Only my eyes remained visible.

Haunted. Hollow. Unfamiliar.

It wasn't just the bandages.

It was the hollowness behind my eyes.

As if the person I'd been—the girl from just days before—had slipped away, leaving only this broken shell behind.

I tried to remember the last time I had seen myself whole—before the crash, before the hospital, before everything changed.

The girl in the mirror back then had been tired, but hopeful. She had been holding a newborn, whispering promises into the dark.

I reached up, trembling, and touched the edge of the bandages.

Would they ever be able to put me back together again?

Would I ever look like myself again?

Tears welled up, but didn't fall.

I didn't have the energy to cry.

The mirror didn't show just bruises and bandages.

It showed everything that had been broken inside of me.

And I stood there, suspended in that moment—watching a stranger in my skin.

The Decision I Didn't Want to Make

Later that day, my brother came to visit.

He walked in quietly, carrying something heavy in his posture.

He sat beside my bed.

For a while, neither of us spoke.

Then, gently, he asked the question no mother should ever have to answer:

Did I want Mom and Jonathan to be placed in the same casket—or did I want Jonathan to have his own?

Even on high doses of morphine, the weight of that question cut through everything else.

I stared at the wall, trying to steady my breath.

The thought of my baby boy in a casket at all was unbearable.

But being with her—his grandmother—felt less lonely somehow.

My voice came out barely above a whisper.

"He can lay with Mom," I said.

It was all I could manage.

A decision made through a haze of heartbreak and pain.

A choice no one should ever have to make.

While grief stayed just out of reach, held back by morphine and shock.

Frozen in Time

Outside my hospital window, the world kept moving.

Traffic flowing.

People laughing.

Clouds drifting across the sky.

But inside that sterile hospital room—inside my broken body—everything had stopped.

Suspended.

Trapped between the girl I had been—and the life I hadn't yet found the strength to face.

I didn't know how to begin again.

But somewhere inside me, breath by breath, I would.

Chapter 20
The Silence Between Us

They weaned me off the morphine slowly, as if softening the blow of returning to real life. But there was no soft landing waiting for me. My childhood home was up for sale. My mother and son were gone. And I was leaving the hospital not to go home, but to live with my sister Alice in the city. I remember being wheeled out the front doors, sunlight too bright, everything too loud. I wasn't ready. But I went anyway—body bandaged, jaw wired shut, heart in pieces.

The year that followed the accident was filled with silent struggles and slow, invisible healing. Sometimes it felt like I was living in the shadow of something too large to name.

The death of my father.

The loss of my mother.

The pain of losing my son.

The trauma of a sexual assault I had never spoken aloud.

Each grief carried its own weight, but together, they created a silence so deep it settled between us—thick, invisible, and everywhere.

But there was something else, too. A silence that wasn't just around me—it lived inside me.

No one talked to me about the accident. No one asked about St. Agnes, or what I had lived through there. No one mentioned my mother or Jonathan.

Grief drifted through every room like smoke, and we all just tried not to breathe it in.

I was almost 19 now. My mouth had been wired shut for twelve weeks. Even after the wires were removed, I lived on soft foods for weeks more before I could chew again.

I had a metal implant to hold my fractured jaw together—a constant, silent reminder of everything that had shattered. Titanium was threaded into the sides of my jawbone where bone had once been, now replaced with wire. It left the entire lower left side of my face and chin without feeling—numb for years. Even now, people sometimes have to tell me when I have food on my chin, because I still can't feel it.

I had suffered a concussion. The entire lower part of my face remained numb for years—a dull, constant absence that reminded me how deeply I'd been broken.

Bright lights gave me headaches for weeks. Crowded rooms made me dizzy. I'd forget what I was saying mid-sentence—then panic, trying to act like I hadn't. I started writing things down—reminders, appointments, names—because my memory wasn't reliable anymore. Not since the crash.

I had a series of appointments with a dental surgeon to adjust the wires and repair my fractured jaw. Some days were unbearable—tightening, clipping, the pressure so intense it made my eyes water. But I was always grateful for the giant fish tank in his office. While he worked, I watched the slow, graceful sweep of fins and bubbles—something calm to focus on when everything else in my life felt fractured.

But none of those physical injuries compared to what I carried inside.

There was a smoldering depression beneath it all—not loud, not dramatic. Just persistent. It dulled the days. It made joy feel unreachable, and grief feel like a slow burn rather than a sharp stab.

And underneath it all, something else lived there. The assault. Still unspoken to everyone but my sister. Still shaping me.

I never talked about it. I didn't even know how. But it was part of me now—woven into my reactions, my relationships, my fears.

It seeped into my marriage—quietly, invisibly, until it shaped everything.

A Place to Heal

After my hospital stay, I moved in with my oldest sister, Alice, and her husband, George. They took care of me until I could drive again and my braces were removed.

Their home became a place of quiet recovery—a space where I could heal at my own fragile pace.

I remember sitting at the kitchen table once, mentioning my mom's name. Alice glanced away, busied herself with wiping crumbs.

"Do you want more tea?" she asked instead. And just like that, a wall rose up between us—the kind built with silence, not words.

One of the sweetest gestures during my recovery came from Alice and George. The day I got my jaw unwired, they planned a big celebration—a full steak barbecue in my honor. They were so proud of how far I had come.

The table was full of laughter, music playing, and plates piled high with thick, juicy steaks hot off the grill.

Only one problem. After twelve weeks of my jaw being wired shut and weeks more of soft foods, my mouth wouldn't open far enough to chew anything.

I smiled politely, sipping a milkshake through a straw while the others dug in. I appreciated every bite I couldn't take. It was thoughtful and loving and completely symbolic of that season of my life—healing, but not quite there yet.

They were so excited for me to eat real food again. But none of us realized that after so long, my jaw had forgotten how to open fully.

I had been living on shakes, watered-down mashed potatoes, and broth sucked through a straw for what felt like an eternity.

Even if, in the end, my celebration meal was a chocolate shake.

Healing wasn't neat. It wasn't fast. But in moments like those, it became a little more bearable.

A Marriage in the '70s

I married a young man two years older than me—someone who embodied the free spirit of the 1970s.

His music, his long hair, his wide-legged jeans. I wore loose clothes and tied my hair in braids.

Marijuana wasn't legal in the United States in 1973—not even close. But it was everywhere. A quiet rebellion woven into the era, rarely acknowledged out loud.

Meanwhile, the world was evolving. The first handheld calculator. The floppy disk. The first video game. McDonald's had just introduced the Egg McMuffin.

The world was moving forward. And I was trying to keep up.

At the time, I thought I had found stability in my husband—someone to build a life with, someone who offered solid ground.

But what I hadn't realized—what wouldn't become clear until much later—was that I had married the extreme opposite of my father.

My father had been steady. Responsible. Rooted in tradition. He believed in structure, in building something lasting.

My husband? He lived for the moment. Untethered. Carefree.

And I didn't see it then, but I understand now— I had been chasing something different.

Something that felt like escape. Maybe I needed that. Maybe I needed someone who didn't remind me of everything I had lost.

Carrying the Past Into the Present

My husband offered a sense of stability when I felt unsteady. But I brought pieces of myself into that marriage—fragments I hadn't yet faced.

It was like carrying an old backpack, filled with things I had never unpacked.

Wounds I thought I had left behind came with me. Quiet, but heavy.

Some nights, I would wake in a cold sweat, heart pounding.

The dreams came in flashes—memories I never wanted to relive.

Hands that didn't belong. A voice I never wanted to hear again. A night that had stolen something from me.

But I would wake. And the house would be still.

And I would tell myself it was over.

But it wasn't.

It stayed with me. Beneath the surface. Waiting.

It made me flinch at certain touches. It made me tense in rooms with closed doors.

And still—I said nothing. That silence lived between us, too.

Not once. Until the day I shattered.

Years later, I would come to understand what I had been living in all along: fight-or-flight. Survival mode, disguised as strength.

I didn't have language for it at the time. But the terror, the numbness, the silence—it all made sense in hindsight.

Back then, I thought I was holding it together. Now I know: I was just holding my breath.

Breaking to Heal

I was newly married. I can't even remember what we argued about. But the frustration boiled up from somewhere deep inside me—a place long sealed off.

Rather than speak, I walked into the kitchen and reached for the china I had inherited after my mother died.

Every bowl. Every cup. Anything breakable.

I threw them to the floor. One by one.

The sharp shatter of glass echoed the chaos inside me.

I watched as it splintered, piece by piece.

Then, I turned to the ceramic lamp my mother had made—delicate and beautiful.

I picked it up. And I threw it down.

It shattered into dust. I stood there, breathless.

I hadn't known how much pain, how much rage, how many buried emotions were waiting to be released.

In the silence that followed, something inside me shifted.

What I hadn't realized until that moment was this: Healing would require breaking first.

A New Kind of Love

Time has a way of carrying us forward, even when we're not ready. The months that followed were uncertain. Each day a tentative step toward healing.

I started noticing the silences in my marriage mirrored the ones inside me—unspoken, unnamed, but always there. The kind of silence that grows between people until it becomes its own presence.

And then—when I least expected it—life surprised me.

A year later, in the middle of all that brokenness, came something whole

A year later, I gave birth to a daughter. Marie.

She arrived with a crown of red hair and the softest cheeks I'd ever touched.

I held her in my arms and pressed my lips to her forehead, feeling something I hadn't felt in a long, long time: Hope.

This baby would live. I could feel it in every cell of my body. I whispered promises to her she couldn't yet understand—but ones I was determined to keep.

When it was time to take her home from the hospital, I refused to take the highway.

The same stretch of road where my mother and Jonathan had died still haunted me.

I made her father take the long way—backroads that twisted through farmland and small-town neighborhoods.

It didn't matter that it took twice as long. I needed that.

I needed a different road. One that didn't carry ghosts.

That detour, for me, was more than distance. It was protection. It was peace. It was my way of choosing life.

Marie's First Challenges

When Marie was born, we had already moved from my hometown—a blessing in its own way. She entered the world differently.

Born without her left forearm.

Doctors ran tests. Countless ones. Searching for answers.

I wrestled with guilt.

Had I done something wrong? Was it my fault?

But when the results came back inconclusive, they finally diagnosed it: Amniotic Band Syndrome.

"Just a rare occurrence," they said.

Her first prosthetic—a tiny, functional hook—was made when she was nine months old.

I remember the first time she used it to grasp a toy.

Such a small moment. But I wept.

She was so proud.

The tap-tap-tap of her prosthetic against the wooden floor as she crawled became music to me.

A rhythm of resilience.

Each sound reminded me: She was strong. She was unstoppable.

Coming Home, Again

Marie's dad became a general contractor, and together we remodeled our first home. After two years, we were ready to sell and return to my hometown.

I believed I was ready.

Our second home was on a quiet street with a cherry tree in the yard.

The blossoms were bright and fragrant, their beauty disarming.

Sometimes I'd bring them inside, placing them in a vase on the kitchen table.

Their scent would fill the house.

A reminder that beauty can still bloom, even after a harsh season.

The city park held a baseball diamond in the heart of town.

I walked past old landmarks:

> The piano recital hall.
>
> The five-and-dime.
>
> The bakery with its sweet window displays.

But one street, I avoided. My father's dental office.

For years, I walked a block around it without even realizing.

Some losses never fade.

But one memory always brought a smile. The banana tree.

My father's harmless prank—wiring green bananas to a tropical plant in our yard.

People would stop, amazed. "How are bananas growing in this climate?" they'd ask.

My father would just shrug, that sparkle in his eye. "Just a little miracle," he'd say, barely hiding his grin.

The town buzzed. Neighbors debated. Even the local paper got involved.

That was my father. Playful. Joyful.

Finding wonder in everyday things.

Even after all I'd lost, that memory remained.

Bright. Alive.

Like a banana ripening where it never should have.

Proof that even in the strangest places, joy could grow.

Chapter 21
The Empty Frame

A New Life, A New Role

It was just a few days a week, but it was exactly what I needed. I became a bank teller.

By that time, my personality was reshaping, coming back to life.

I had the gift of gab—and back then, all teller drawers had to balance before anyone could go home. If your drawer was off by even ten cents, the entire staff had to stay late until the error was found.

Mine was always off.

A few pennies here, a nickel there—a dime when I was really distracted.

Because I talked too much.

I loved chatting with customers, exchanging stories, laughing when I should have been double-checking my math.

Impatient glances from the other tellers came at least once a week, their glares pressing into the back of my neck.

"Not again," they'd groan.

The bank president noticed.

"You're great with people," he told me one afternoon, "but let's be honest, balancing a drawer is not your strong suit."

I laughed, a little embarrassed. "I guess I talk too much while I'm counting."

"Exactly!" he said, grinning. "That's why I need you somewhere you can use that charm—without worrying about nickels and dimes."

And just like that, I was moved to new accounts, where my energy and friendliness could shine.

I flourished in that role, finding a sense of confidence and independence that contrasted with the uncertainty growing in my marriage.

At the bank, I was valued. Seen.

And I made a lifelong friend there—Joyce.

Her friendship became an anchor during those early days when I was just learning to step into myself again.

At home, I felt myself disappearing. Piece by piece.

But the best part of every day was opening the front door and hearing the sound of tiny footsteps racing toward me.

Marie had been staying with a good friend while I worked—just a few days a week, enough to get me out of the house and around adults.

She was my happy place.

The moment I walked through the door, she'd come running into my arms, grinning from ear to ear.

It was the kind of joy that reminded me why I kept going.

Some nights, I would sit alone at the kitchen table, tracing my fingers along the wood grain, wondering how two versions of myself could exist at once—One thriving.

One fading.

The contrast was stark.

And I wondered how long I could keep balancing between the two worlds before one consumed me entirely.

The Walk to City Hall

One afternoon, during my lunch break, I decided to take a walk and found myself heading toward City Hall.

The town had changed, but City Hall stood the same—its tall columns weathered but unmoved, standing as silent witnesses to the passing years.

The air was crisp, carrying the faint scent of rain from earlier in the day.

Leaves skittered across the sidewalk, their rustling the only sound as I approached the familiar old building.

Each step felt heavier than the last, as if—deep down—I knew something inside was waiting to shake me.

The Missing Picture

As I stepped inside, the receptionist glanced up.

"Can I help you?" she asked, polite but distracted.

I hesitated. "I just... I was looking for my father's picture. It used to hang right here. My father was a mayor, and I wanted to see his picture."

She nodded, pointing down the hall. "They're still in the same place. Feel free to take a look."

My feet carried me forward, past decades of faces, each framed in neat rows—a silent tribute to those who had led our town.

And then—I stopped.

A cold wave rolled through me.

His name was there.

But above it—An empty frame.

I blinked. Once. Twice.

A hollow ache bloomed in my chest.

An emptiness so sharp it felt physical—as if someone had reached into the wall and pulled him out of memory itself.

I blinked again, willing the image to change.

But it was gone.

Erased.

The Realization

"Excuse me," I turned back to the receptionist, my voice barely above a whisper. "Why is my father's picture missing?"

She frowned, flipping through a file on her desk. "I'm not sure. It could be it was taken down for reframing."

"Or maybe someone just forgot him," I muttered under my breath, my throat tightening.

A memory surfaced, untouched by time—

The Flashback

I was 12 years old, my hand tucked in his as we climbed the steps to City Hall on the day he was first elected mayor.

He was beaming, his excitement radiating from him.

"This is history, kiddo," he had said, squeezing my hand. "We're part of something bigger than ourselves."

I had looked up at him, proud, watching the way he carried himself— his shoulders straight, his stride purposeful.

In that moment, I believed that this place would always hold him.

That the walls would always remember.

The Collapse & the Weight of Everyone Knowing

But now, standing here years later, it felt like the town had erased him from its history, leaving only an empty space where he once belonged.

Maybe that is what grief does.

It doesn't just mourn the person lost—it mourns the frame they once fit into.

I stood frozen, emotions crashing over me in waves—grief, anger, disbelief.

It felt as though the ground beneath me had shifted, as though time had betrayed me.

My father had once walked these halls, his presence woven into the town's history.

And now—there was only emptiness where he should have been.

A dizzying lightheadedness swept over me.

I staggered.

The world tilted—And then—Blackness.

Small Towns Never Keep Secrets

My hometown was just small enough that someone at City Hall knew I worked at the bank.

Through the bank, they contacted my husband.

And suddenly—everyone knew.

By the time I woke up, I wasn't just a woman who had fainted in City Hall.

I was the woman who had fainted in City Hall because her father's picture was missing.

The woman whose grief was now on full display for an entire town.

There was no hiding in a town like this.

Every glance, every whispered conversation stitched me into a story I hadn't chosen to tell.

The hardest part wasn't just the disorientation when I opened my eyes again.

It was the knowing looks at the bank the next day.

It was the soft, sympathetic smiles that made my skin crawl.

It was the whispers I wasn't meant to hear.

"Did you hear what happened?"

"I can't imagine... after everything she's been through."

"They really should have never taken his picture down."

Grief is heavy.

But grief that everyone else can see?

That is unbearable.

I didn't know it at the time, but the missing portrait had cracked something open.

It stirred emotions I hadn't even realized were buried—grief, loss, abandonment—and once they surfaced, they didn't go back quietly.

At the bank, I was seen. At home, I was disappearing.

And here—at City Hall—I was laid bare for all to witness.

And it wasn't just about him.

It was the terrifying truth:

None of us are remembered the way we think we will be.

Not by the places we loved.

Not by the people we left behind.

Only by the echoes we leave in their hearts—if we're lucky.

Chapter 22

One Block at a Time

Days turned into weeks.
Weeks turned into months since I had fallen apart at City Hall and could no longer return to my job at the bank.

I remember the moment vividly—standing there, my breath shallow, my vision blurring as my body shook.

The room felt too bright, the murmurs of people around me like distant echoes.

My chest tightened, as if something heavy were pressing down on it.

And then, everything collapsed.

Something had stirred in my subconscious. It was as if Pandora's box had been opened—grief, trauma, memories I had locked away—and I couldn't close it again.

After that day, I couldn't go back.

I couldn't face the world I once navigated so easily.

I would sit for long stretches, staring at nothing, my mind an empty void.

I had become numb. And I didn't know why.

I had become depressed.

And I didn't understand it.

Conversations around me felt distant, like I was trapped behind an invisible wall.

Even the smallest tasks felt impossible.

I thought about how I used to scoop my daughter into my arms, how I used to laugh and twirl her around.

Now, I could barely lift my head when she called for me.

Losing Confidence

It wasn't just my job I lost—I lost my independence.

One day, I sat at a red light, gripping the steering wheel, heart pounding.

I stared at the colors—red, green, yellow—and suddenly, I couldn't remember what they meant.

I froze, paralyzed by fear.

It was as if my mind had abandoned me.

Terror gripped my chest as horns blared behind me, impatient drivers shouting. I knew I had to move, but I couldn't trust myself.

I quit driving.

Every time I tried, everything outside the windshield rushed at me too fast—cars, buildings, traffic lights—all blurring together in a chaotic swirl. My brain couldn't process the movement.

That was the day I gave up.

I couldn't do it anymore.

With every failed attempt, I lost more confidence—not just in driving, but in myself.

I felt useless. Broken. Incapable.

My backpack of grief and heartache was full. But I didn't know it then.

A Child's Love

Marie was four and a half years old by then.

She was always trying to get her mama to come outside and play, to spend time with her.

One day, she came running in, her face lit up with excitement.

"Mama, Mama, Mama! I have been outside riding my worm!"

She meant her green plastic worm—a ride-on toy she could bounce on, hopping across the yard.

It was her favorite thing in the world.

That afternoon, she was so full of delight, so eager to tell me something important.

"Mama, Mama! I have been riding my worm so that you could have energy."

Her words were so innocent, so full of love.

My heart ached.

She was trying to help me in her sweet, childlike way.

But it didn't help.

I smiled for her, but inside, I felt nothing.

I wanted to reach for the joy in her eyes, but it was like trying to hold onto smoke.

The World Had Turned Brown

Some days, I would step outside and look at the cherry tree in our yard.

It had once been my favorite.

In years past, its blossoms had brought me joy—soft pinks and whites filling the air with the fragrance of spring.

I used to sit beneath it, watching the petals drift like snowflakes.

One year, I had even lifted Marie up so she could run her tiny fingers over the soft petals.

But now—

Everything was brown.

It was like living in a photograph faded by time—colors once vivid now washed in sorrow.

The blossoms were brown.

The world around me had turned to shades of lifeless sepia.

No matter where I looked, everything felt dull, faded, empty.

The air smelled stale.

Even the laughter of my daughter seemed distant, like an echo from a world I could no longer reach.

Step by Step

We sold that house and moved just a few blocks away.

Bit by bit, I started to have energy again.

But it took work.

At first, I could only walk one block.

Then two.

Then three.

Healing wasn't a sunrise.

It was a series of tiny, stubborn steps—each one defying the part of me that wanted to give up.

Every day, I would push myself outside, forcing my legs to move, whispering a mantra to myself:

"Every day, in every way, I get better, better, and better."

At first, the words felt empty.

But I kept repeating them.

Even when I didn't believe them.

And slowly, something shifted.

A Friend Who Showed Up

I made friends with Susan, who lived just three houses down.

She had children close to Marie's age.

Her kindness was effortless, patient, unwavering.

Susan took me under her wing.

She helped me face my fears.

She got me used to riding in a car again—one block at a time.

Then two.

Then around the whole neighborhood.

She never rushed me.

If I couldn't make it out the door, she would sit with me at the dining room table, listening as I poured out my anxieties.

She proved to me, day after day, that I wasn't a burden.

That I was worthy of help.

I had been to doctors who only sent me home, telling me it was all in my head. They ran MRIs and CT scans, thinking maybe the car accident had caused something.

It had.

But not the kind of damage the medical world could see.

The Cherry Blossoms Bloomed Again

A year passed.

Susan had been helping me every step of the way.

And then, one afternoon in the spring, we happened to drive past my old house.

The one with the cherry tree I had loved so much.

It was springtime.

My heart pounded as I looked out the window.

And then—I saw it.

The cherry blossoms were pink again.

No longer brown.

My breath caught.

Warmth spread through my chest.

Tears pricked my eyes.

I turned to Susan, my voice trembling.

"I think I'm ready to start living again."

She smiled, reaching over to squeeze my hand.

"I knew you would be."

The world had color again.

And for the first time in a long time, I believed in the possibility of joy.

The Gift of Friendship

Susan didn't just help me get in a car again.

She helped me get back into life.

She showed up day after day, without hesitation.

She took me on small adventures—

A quick grocery run.

A simple coffee outing.

A walk through the park.

Each one felt like a step toward reclaiming myself.

She never treated me like I was fragile.

She never made me feel like I was too much.

She just showed up.

And that saved me.

I had even started going to Marie's father's softball games, sitting in the bleachers, cheering him on—pretending I was just another normal person out in the world again.

But there were cracks in the marriage.

And I know—living with me, watching me check out of life—couldn't have been easy for him.

Now, whenever I see cherry blossoms, I think of that spring day in the park.

I think of Susan's hand gently resting on mine as petals fell around us.

It's a reminder that something beautiful can bloom after a long, cold season.

In my life's darkest winter, Susan was the warmth and light that encouraged me to grow again.

I hope she knows just how much she changed my life.

I've told her "thank you" more times than I can count—But it still doesn't feel like enough.

Because how do you properly thank someone for saving you in all the ways a person can be saved?

In the end, I realized—True friendship can be as vital as air.

And thanks to Susan, I could finally breathe again.

See the world again.

Eventually, the time came to say goodbye.

Susan had been my steady light in the darkest of seasons, and I will forever be grateful for the way she showed up—again and again—with nothing but love and quiet strength.

She had lit the way when I couldn't find it myself.

And though miles would separate us, her kindness would live in me forever—a reminder that sometimes, one person's unwavering belief can rebuild another's world.

She had helped me believe in life again.

But life was shifting once more.

My husband's business had failed. A friend had encouraged him to come east—promising opportunity and the chance to start over.

He thought getting away from my hometown might help me heal.

And so, we sold the house and packed up what we had, preparing to rent in a small town tucked deep in snow country.

It was the beginning of another chapter—quiet, cold, and unfamiliar.

And as we pulled away, I carried Susan's love with me like a lantern in the dark.

Chapter 23
Change

The wind howled as we stepped out of the car, whipping snowflakes around us like tiny daggers.

The towering ponderosa pines stood like silent sentinels, their branches heavy with ice, bending under the weight of winter.

The crisp air carried the scent of pine and wood smoke, sharp and clean—so different from the damp earth and cherry blossoms I had left behind.

The change in scenery was drastic—gone were the soft pinks of spring, replaced by vast stretches of white, a world blanketed in cold silence.

I had traded blossoms for barrenness, warmth for silence.

Each breath was sharp and crisp, stinging my cheeks, making my lungs burn in a way that felt both fresh and unfamiliar.

I had looked forward to this change.

Before the move, Susan had helped me heal, had guided me back to a version of myself that was ready for something new.

Now, we were a family of five—Marie, Ann, and baby Rose.

I would bundle up Rose and carry her outside, her tiny hands grasping at the air as her sisters squealed, kicking up flurries of snow.

I should have felt whole.

I should have felt happy.

But beneath the surface, something was shifting.

Healing wasn't linear.

I had stitched myself back together—but some seams were starting to pull apart.

Finding Joy Amidst the Cold

The first morning after we arrived, I pulled back the curtain and gasped.

Overnight, the world had transformed.

Snow piled high against the porch, the trees stood heavy with ice, and the sky stretched into an endless blue expanse.

I opened the door, and a blast of crisp air rushed in, carrying the scent of pine and fresh winter. Marie and Ann squealed, their excitement spilling into the wind as they dashed outside, their laughter disappearing into the white wilderness.

Adjusting to life in snow country was a challenge.

The roads were different, the pace of life slower, dictated by unpredictable weather.

I still wasn't driving, but that didn't bother me.

My days were filled with:

Bundling up children.

Hot cocoa by the fire.

The rhythm of snowflakes tapping against the window.

One afternoon, Marie begged to build a snow fort.

Marie and Ann shrieked with laughter, leaving deep footprints in the snow, kicking up flurries of white.

For a moment, watching them, I felt it too—That simple, untamed joy of childhood.

I let out a laugh, unexpected and real, as I held Rose and plopped down next to them.

The cold air stung my cheeks as I slid down the hill, my laughter mixing with theirs.

For a moment, nothing else mattered.

But moments like these were fleeting.

The Cracks Beneath the Surface

The house we moved into felt warm and safe, a stark contrast to the icy world outside.

The fire crackled, filling the rooms with the scent of burning pine.

The smell of cinnamon candles mixed with the rich aroma of hot cocoa.

Snow piled high against the windows, creating a sense of quiet isolation—but also peace.

To outsiders, we looked like a picture-perfect family:

Three beautiful daughters.

A home in the snow.

Traditions that made the holidays feel warm and full.

But traditions can be a mask, too—covering over the fractures with ribbon and light.

Behind closed doors, the distance between my husband and myself grew wider.

The move had not brought us closer together. Just the opposite.

The silences became heavier.

Some nights, I lay awake next to a man who felt more like a stranger, listening to the wind howl outside, wondering how we had made it this far.

I wanted to be happy.

But I felt myself slipping away, piece by piece.

How much longer could I pretend?

One night, the wind was so fierce it rattled the windows, shaking the house to its foundation.

I wrapped myself in a blanket, staring at the fire while the storm raged outside.

My husband sat across the room, lost in his own thoughts, the silence between us stretching long and unforgiving.

Outside, the world was buried under feet of snow.

Inside, I felt just as trapped.

The Day of Decision

And then, one day—the decision came and after Marie's school bus dropped her off and while the girls' father was at work, I picked up the phone.

My hands trembled as I dialed.

Each number felt like a leap across a canyon.

Leah answered. She had been at my house several weeks before and had told me, "If it ever gets bad enough, come to my house," a forty-minute drive away.

"Hey, you," she said, her voice warm as ever.

"Are you okay?"

I swallowed hard.

"No."

Silence.

Then a deep sigh.

"I knew this day would come," she said. "I just didn't think it would be so soon."

Tears welled in my eyes.

"Me neither."

Leaving, But Not Leaving the Snow Behind

Unlike before, I wasn't leaving the snow behind.

Leah's house had snow too.

We both lived in what was called the high desert, our altitude around 3,200 feet.

The winters were just as cold.

The snow just as deep.

But this time, the snow wasn't what I was leaving behind.

This time, I was leaving a marriage that had long been unraveling.

The girls were confused as I hurried to gather our things.

Ann clutched her stuffed animal tightly.

"Where are we going, Mommy?"

"We're going to Aunt Leah's, sweetheart. Just for a little visit," I replied, forcing a calm smile.

Marie stood frozen, her backpack dangling from one shoulder.

"What about Dad?"

I met Marie's eyes, brushing a strand of hair behind her ear.

"We'll be okay," I whispered, forcing a smile that didn't quite reach my eyes.

"I just need us to go, sweetheart. Trust me."

I fastened Rose's seatbelt firmly in her booster seat and handed her favorite doll to her.

I glanced at Marie through the rearview mirror.

Her arms were folded tightly across her lap, her face turned toward the window, frowning.

The confusion, the weight of the unknown—it was all there in her reflection.

My heart ached.

She deserved answers I couldn't fully give her yet.

White Knuckles on the Wheel

I hadn't driven in years.

But this time, I had no choice.

The car was packed, the girls buckled in, and Leah's house was forty minutes away.

My hands gripped the wheel so tightly my knuckles turned white.

Every intersection felt overwhelming, every turn a battle against the anxiety that had kept me from driving for so long.

The road stretched ahead, slick with ice, the mountains looming in the distance.

My heart pounded with every mile.

Sweat beaded at the base of my neck despite the cold.

Every mile was a victory.

Every breath was a prayer.

But I kept my foot on the gas.

And I kept telling myself—

I can do this.

I can do this.

With every passing mile, the fear didn't disappear—but I didn't let it win.

Arrival at Leah's

Leah met us at the door before I even had time to knock.

The second I stepped inside, she wrapped her arms around me, holding me tight.

"I'm so glad you're here," she murmured.

"I've got you. You're safe now."

The words broke something inside me.

For the first time all day, I let myself believe it—We made it. We made it safely.

I could breathe.

Change wasn't easy.

It was terrifying.

But it was the first step toward becoming someone new.

Chapter 24
Chinese Fire Drill

The car came to a screeching halt at the red light, tires skidding across pavement.

Before the car even settled, we threw open the doors and bolted into the street, the icy wind biting our cheeks as our laughter met the air..

Marie and Ann's giggles cut through the cold air, their shoes slipping and sliding as they raced around the car.

I scrambled toward the driver's seat, breathless, trying to beat Leah there. She was fast, but I was faster.

The second I flung the door shut, I slammed my foot on the gas, and we peeled off just as the light turned green—our laughter echoing through the car.

Leah was laughing so hard she was crying, gripping the dashboard.

"You little sneak!" she gasped between breaths. "You totally stole my seat!"

"You snooze, you lose!" I shot back, wiping tears from my eyes.

Ann leaned forward from the backseat, breathless with giggles.

"Mama, do it again!"

I glanced at Leah, and for a split second, we were kids again—best friends since first grade, whispering secrets under desks, playing hopscotch in the sun.

For the first time in so long, I felt light. Alive.

The past hadn't disappeared, but for a moment, it wasn't so heavy.

Leah's son, Jason, sat in the backseat, arms crossed, shaking his head.

"You guys are ridiculous," he muttered, unimpressed.

He hadn't even bothered getting out of the car.

While Marie and Ann loved the chaos, Jason stayed put, waiting for our nonsense to end.

Leah wiped away a tear, catching her breath.

"Oh, come on, Jason," she teased. "Not even a little fun?"

He sighed dramatically.

"I'm just saying, this is a terrible strategy for survival."

Marie burst into laughter.

"Jason, it's not about survival. It's about fun!"

He let out another long-suffering sigh.

"Right. Of course. Because running in traffic is always fun."

Leah and I exchanged a glance and dissolved into laughter again.

Jason shook his head, muttering under his breath, while Marie and Ann cheered for another round.

The laughter didn't end when we pulled into Leah's driveway.

It carried into the house—into the kitchen, the living room, the very walls themselves.

The Heart of Leah's House

Laughter filled the house.

The kitchen became a space of joy, of trial and error, of endless silliness.

Leah was always up for trying something new, which led to some truly memorable creations during her gluten-free, sugar-free phase.

The things she baked—the odd textures, the bizarre flavors, the unpredictable colors—kept us in stitches.

We never knew what shade of green or gray might emerge from the oven next, but the fun of it all was what truly mattered.

No matter what, the house was filled with warmth.

With laughter.

With life.

Old Tricks, New Memories

Leah had always been the smart one.

The studious one.

The composed and poised one.

And me?

I was the one pulling tricks when she least expected it.

I remembered in high school, passing her in the halls—jumping up and down, waving my arms

like a lunatic outside her trigonometry class.

But Leah?

She wouldn't flinch.

She would sit there, eyes forward, ignoring me with monk-like discipline.

One time, I snuck into her classroom before the bell rang and wrote "HELP ME" in big letters on her notebook.

When she opened it, she calmly ripped out the page, balled it up, and kept writing.

I was outside the door, dying with laughter.

Some things never changed.

The Dream House Built from Loss

Leah's home—hers and Bill's dream—was perched at the edge of a rocky cliff, surrounded by towering ponderosa pines and the earthy scent of the outdoors.

Floor-to-ceiling windows overlooked three mountaintops called Hope, Faith, and Charity.

Bill had been a LearJet pilot. Just before the crash that took his life, he and Leah had finished the plans for their dream home.

After he died, Leah—strong and steady—took those plans and built the house they had dreamed of together.

She had taken heartbreak and, with her own two hands, built something breathtaking—a reminder that dreams can survive even the fiercest storms.

The sunsets and sunrises painted the sky in fiery oranges, soft pinks, and the kind of blue you only see in dreams.

The Walks That Rebuilt Me

Each day, we took long walks along a mile-and-a-half stretch of road that looped through the high desert hills.

The air was crisp with pine and juniper, and with every step, we talked—About life.

About dreams.

About the past.

About the future.

Some days, I felt lighter, shedding the weight I had carried for so long.

Other days, the burdens returned, pressing down with familiar heaviness.

Healing wasn't a straight path.

It felt like two steps forward and one step back.

But with each walk, each conversation, I stitched myself a little more whole.

Leah listened without judgment, offering both laughter and quiet understanding.

She reminded me of my strength on the days I doubted myself.

Loss had threaded through both our stories.

And yet here we were.

Together.

The sound of our footsteps on the pavement became a rhythm of renewal—a steady beat reminding me that I was moving forward, even if it didn't always feel like it.

With every sunrise that met us on our path—through those massive windows, across the rolling hills—I realized I was no longer just surviving.

I was truly starting to live again.

Chapter 25
Finding My Voice

The divorce was long, drawn-out, and ugly.

I sat in the courtroom, my hands clenched in my lap, my fingers ice-cold despite the heat rising in my chest.

The sound of rustling papers filled the room as the judge shifted in his seat, his eyes serious, scanning the documents before him.

Every time his gaze flickered toward me, I held my breath.

The courtroom felt cold.

Too cold.

A shiver ran down my spine, though I knew it wasn't just from the temperature.

It reminded me of City Hall—of the day I found my father's picture missing from the wall.

The same hollow ache settled in my chest. A reminder that things—people—could be erased.

Rewritten. Made to disappear as if they never mattered.

But this time, I wasn't just watching someone disappear from history.

I was fighting to make sure I stayed in it—for my daughters, for myself.

I thought about the year that led to this moment:

- The anxiety.

- The sleepless nights.

- The weight loss.

- The exhaustion of constantly worrying someone might take my daughters away from me.

And now, here I was.

Fighting for them.

I had watched him across the courtroom—stoic, composed, unflinching.

I didn't know if I could take one more disappointment.

I had held everything in—my fear, my anger, my hope—for so long.

When the ruling was finally made in my favor, the world shifted beneath me.

The dam inside me broke.

Tears streamed down my face as I clutched my hands to my chest.

I had won.

I was not mentally incompetent. I was not an unfit parent.

I was capable of caring for my children.

I got to be their mother.

Their dad would have them every other weekend and on designated holidays.

The divorce was final.

And then, outside the courthouse, I couldn't help myself.

I asked Dean, "Why? Why did you drag me through the court system for an entire year?"

He looked at me without hesitation and said, "I wanted to prove to the girls that I loved them."

What? I said, caught off guard.

I stared at him, stunned. That was his justification?

I shook my head in disbelief, dumbfounded, and walked away.

No more words.

Just space.

And resolve.

I should have felt victorious.

Instead, I just felt... emptied out.

Like I had crossed a finish line with nothing left in the tank.

As much as Leah's home had given us safety and stability, the past still lingered. Ghosts don't pack up just because the papers are signed.

The Dutch Door

One Sunday afternoon, my ex-husband brought the girls back—just as he always did every other weekend.

They ran toward me, their laughter like bells in the air.

Leah's house had a Dutch door—the kind where the top and bottom halves opened separately.

As I hugged them tight and sent them inside, their father muttered something under his breath. A rude, cutting remark—meant to hit below the surface.

Leah and I used to joke that she was the composed one and I was the wild one.

But that day, at that Dutch door, I discovered a different kind of strength.

Something in me snapped—but not in a way that unraveled.

In a way that finally, finally solidified.

"Dean," I called after him.

He turned, expecting something else—Maybe an apology.

Maybe a plea.

Maybe weakness.

Instead, I looked him square in the eye and said:

"Fuck you."

The words burned on my tongue.

Hot.

Searing.

Unapologetic.

I didn't flinch.

I didn't explain.

I didn't walk it back.

I had meant it.

Two weeks earlier, when he dropped the girls off, he had told me God sent him a vision—a warning that one of our daughters would be killed in a car accident if I didn't come back to him.

That day, I had stayed silent.

But not this time.

This time, I drew the line.

This time, I stood in my truth and didn't look away.

One more—"Fuck you."

It rang out as I slammed and locked the top half of the Dutch door. I turned and put my back against it.

Breathing hard.

Heart pounding

But for the first time in a long, long time— It felt good

It wasn't rage.

It was reclamation.

It was the sound of my own strength returning—loud, unapologetic, and mine.

And it felt so good.

After he drove away, I stood with my back against the door, breathing hard.

But I wasn't done yet

A few hours later—just before the sun dipped below the hills—I laced up my sneakers and walked the 1.5-mile loop Leah and I always walk together.

This time, I walked it alone

And the whole way, I muttered one word, over and over again under my breath:

"Fuck. Fuck. Fuck."

I said it like a mantra. Like a hymn. Like a prayer I was finally allowed to pray.

I didn't care who saw me.

I didn't care who heard

It wasn't rage. It was release.

And it felt good

So damn good.

Chapter 26
What We Carry

The day came when it was time to move out of Leah's house.

She helped me pack up the last of my things—taping up boxes, carefully wrapping dishes, making sure nothing was forgotten. The kids were gone with their dad for the weekend, leaving just the two of us.

Leah helped me unpack at my new apartment, her presence making the transition easier, less overwhelming. But when the last box was set down and she stood in the doorway, ready to leave, I felt something tighten in my chest.

"Well," she said, dusting off her hands. "You're officially on your own."

I forced a smile.

"Thanks for everything, Leah. I don't know what I would have done without you."

Leah and I had been friends since first grade. I still remember the day we met. I realized my pencil was too dull to use, so I glanced around the nearby desks for a solution—and spotted her.

Hair perfect. Dress crisp. White anklets. Black Mary Janes. She looked like a picture in a storybook. I, on the other hand, had just come in from recess—my hair a mess, my knees scraped, my socks already sliding down.

There was a pencil sitting neatly on her desk. So I did what any messy-haired six-year-old would do: I walked right up and took it.

I had barely started writing when it was yanked right out of my fingers. Leah stood beside me, reclaiming her pencil without saying a word. I looked up at her—braver than I felt—and from that day on, we were inseparable. Opposites from the beginning. And friends for life.

We had no idea then how much we would walk each other through. I lost my father first. Then she lost hers, followed by her mother. And later, Bill, her husband a Learjet pilot. Grief didn't divide us—it braided our lives together. Loss became one more thread in the fabric of our friendship. A quiet understanding that needed no explanation.

She pulled me into a hug, squeezing tight.

"You're going to be okay. You know that, right?"

I nodded, but I wasn't sure I believed it.

I whispered, "You're the Wind Beneath My Wings."

It was our movie—Beaches. We had sobbed through it together in the theater years earlier, and claimed it as ours.

Then Leah left.

The door clicked shut behind her.

The sound echoed through the empty rooms, louder than it should have been.

I had never lived alone before. Not really.

I had gone from my mother's house, to my sister Alice's, to being married to Dean.

This was the first time I stood on my own, without someone nearby to carry part of the weight.

Now, it was just me.

I stood there for a long time, not moving. Not unpacking. Just standing still—feeling what aloneness felt like.

It wasn't loud or dramatic. It was a quiet ache. A low hum in my bones.

Not loneliness exactly, but something deeper.

The beginning of a life where I would have to hold my own weight—and learn how to sit inside the silence.

The stillness was unnerving. I stood in it for as long as I could.

Then I walked to the kitchen and turned on the radio—just to hear another voice in the room.

Not to drown the silence completely. Just enough to feel a little less alone.

It was a simple apartment—nothing fancy. Pale green walls. Drapes that didn't quite reach the floor. A couch I had just purchased at a garage sale, sitting stark and alone in an otherwise empty living room.

I walked through each room thinking of the things I would still need to purchase.

A toaster.

Bath towels.

I had my oak antique dining room table—the one I had sanded down with the girls' dad and refinished. A faint smile crossed my lips remembering the divorce tug-of-war over that table.

I got it.

I stood at the kitchen counter making a list of things I still needed.

Then, I noticed it—A laundry basket sitting in the corner.

I sighed and walked over to unpack it, pulling out the last of the dish towels and oven mitts from the bottom.

And then—Tucked beneath the folded towels and a sweater, I found a thin manila folder, hidden away like a secret.

I picked it up, frowning, turning it over in my hands. It had to be Leah's—her laundry baskets had been used while we packed. I assumed it had just gotten mixed in.

But then I opened it.

The Final Words

I wasn't expecting it.

But there they were—Bill's final words. A transcript. The final communication between Leah's husband and the control tower. His last exchange. His last moments.

And not just his. A co-pilot had been with him that day.

Two voices inside the cockpit. Two men steering forward together.

Their final moments had been recorded—every clipped syllable, every calm instruction, every attempt at control as the plane neared the mountainside. Up until the second life no longer existed.

My breath caught.

Their voices on paper—the pilot and the co-pilot—felt like echoes from another world. I read them aloud in a whisper, as if I could somehow keep them tethered.

I clutched the folder to my chest.

Two Pilots, Two Endings

This wasn't mine to read.

I wasn't meant to hold this.

And yet, there I was, on the floor of my new apartment, listening to the final echoes of two lives—Bill's and his co-pilot's—who had no idea they were flying toward their last moments.

Who believed they would land.

Who believed they still had time.

And then suddenly, I wasn't just thinking about them.

I was thinking about my mother.

She had been the pilot of our car that day.

She, too, had been steering forward—believing she would arrive.

Believing there was still time.

In the seconds before impact, I know she must have tried to save us.

Just like Bill must have.

Just like his co-pilot.

Just like any soul who sees the end before they feel ready.

The Weight of What Remains

I had spent so many years trying to move forward—trying to let go.

But that's the thing about grief. It's not something you leave behind.

It's something you carry—in small, hidden ways.

In a banana tree outside a dental office.

In the smell of cherry blossoms.

In the whisper of a name you no longer say out loud but still hear in your heart.

And now, in a manila folder at the bottom of a laundry basket.

Moving Forward Alone, But Not Empty

I sat with the folder a long while.

Then I closed it—gently, reverently—and set it aside.

There are things we carry with us even when we think we've let them go.

And maybe that's not a burden.

Maybe it's the evidence that love doesn't leave.

That loss isn't just about absence—it's also about presence.

What remains. What whispers. What shapes us as we continue forward.

I stood up.

Wiped my eyes.

And took a deep breath.

It was time to keep going—not empty, but carrying something real.

Chapter 27
Cracks in the Surface

I hadn't cried through the divorce.

Not when I packed up the house.

Not when I signed the papers.

Not even when the silence of my bedroom pressed against me like a second skin.

I had just moved into my own apartment for the first time in my life.

No safety net. No one in the next room.

Eight months later, I lost the one job I had managed to land—fired after a sharp exchange with the owner that I couldn't bring myself to regret or explain.

I was unraveling in small, quiet ways.

Ways that didn't make headlines.

Ways that didn't stop the world—but stopped me.

The cracks had already begun.

And the weight of holding everything together was starting to show.

I hadn't slept in nights.

Maybe longer than I wanted to admit.

The quiet of the house, on weekends when the girls were with their father, a comfort, had become unbearable. The nights stretched long and haunted, filled with racing thoughts and an ache I couldn't soothe. I was exhausted, but sleep wouldn't come.

Then came the afternoon I couldn't find my car.

I had gone to the grocery store for a few things—just a short errand. I remember standing in the checkout line and realizing I didn't even know what I had put in my cart. When I stepped outside, the sun hit me like a spotlight, and everything spun.

The parking lot stretched out in all directions. I couldn't remember where I'd parked.

I couldn't remember anything.

I froze. My heart began pounding so hard I thought it would crack my ribs. My hands shook. I looked around and saw people walking, talking, pushing carts—but it all felt far away, like I was underwater.

I couldn't breathe.

I was unraveling. Right there between rows of sedans and shopping carts.

And what scared me the most—more than losing my breath or forgetting where I parked—was the creeping realization that I had been here before.

Years earlier, when life had felt too heavy to bear, I gave up driving altogether. For seven years, I'd relied on others to get me where I needed to go. I had lost not only my confidence but my independence. It was Susan who had gently, patiently helped me reclaim small joys again—rides to the beach, afternoons of laughter, slow mornings with purpose. With her by my side, I had climbed out of that fog.

But now, standing in that parking lot with my keys clenched in my fist and panic flooding my chest, I felt the old fear creeping back .

I couldn't go back.

Not after how far I'd come.

That's what made it worse.

The weight of what I stood to lose again.

And how close I was to losing it.

I spotted a pay phone near the edge of the lot and stumbled toward it, clutching my purse with both hands like it was the only thing holding me together. I called a friend—one of the few I trusted—and somehow got the words out. She came and picked me up without asking questions.

She took me straight to my doctor's office.

I didn't have an appointment, but I sat in the waiting room for over an hour, trying to look normal. Trying not to cry. Trying not to fall apart.

When he finally called me in, I could barely look at him.

"I think I have cancer," I told him.

I explained about the hard lump on my lower back—how I could feel it every time I sat down, especially when I drove.

He gently examined me, then looked me in the eye.

"That's your tailbone," he said softly. "You've just lost so much weight it's sticking out now."

I was down to a hundred pounds.

He didn't laugh. He didn't brush it off.

This was the same doctor who had been trying to help me manage my anxiety for months.

He knew I wasn't sleeping.

He had seen the weight drop, the energy fade.

I had been in his office regularly, trying to hold things together with sheer will and the thinnest thread of hope.

But by now, even that wasn't working.

I had no appetite. No rest. No reserves left.

He sat quietly for a moment, then said, "I want to make a few calls. Can you come back tomorrow?"

I nodded. I didn't ask questions.

I was too hollow to push back.

The next day, I sat across from him again.

He didn't waste words.

"You're not okay," he said. "You need more support than I can give you here."

He told me he was sending me to a major hospital in the city—three hours away.

They had a psychiatric unit. A good one.

"I want you to go tomorrow," he said. "You'll be admitted right away."

My throat tightened.

"What about my girls?" I whispered.

"You'll need to find someone you trust to care for them while you're gone," he said gently. "And let your job know you'll need to take some time off."

I almost laughed at that.

There was no job.

No schedule to clear. Just one more thread that had already unraveled.

But what weighed on me most wasn't the job.

It was the girls.

I had just spent a year in court fighting to prove I was a fit mother. Every motion, every affidavit, every appearance—it all led to one thing: I had won custody.

They were mine to raise, protect, and keep safe.

The idea of stepping away—even for a short time—felt like surrender. But I knew better.

This wasn't giving up.

This was choosing to fight a different way.

I nodded slowly, the words falling over me like warm rain and cold wind all at once.

"Do you have someone who can drive you?"

"Yes," I said. "Leah."

"Good," he said. "Let's not wait."

It was happening.

It was real.

I wasn't just tired or overwhelmed.

I was disappearing.

And someone had finally seen me.

That night, I sat in my bedroom, looking around at the life I had tried so hard to hold together.

I thought about my girls—what they needed, what I hadn't been able to give.

I thought about what it meant to leave, even for a little while.

But beneath all of that was something quieter.

Something closer to relief.

Because for the first time in a long time, I wasn't pretending.

I wasn't powering through.

I was letting go.

And maybe—just maybe—that was the beginning of coming back.

Chapter 28

The Quiet Before
the Storm

It was dark outside and cold.

Winter in the Pacific Northwest had a way of pressing in, heavy and gray.

Droplets of rain clung to the windows of my third-floor hospital room.

The world beyond blurred into smudges of gray and dim yellow streetlights.

Hope felt just as far away.

The air inside smelled faintly of disinfectant, and I hadn't expected to feel so overwhelmed.

The locked doors. The locked windows. The absence of anything sharp.

It all made the admission feel more drastic than I was prepared for.

I remember thinking—Do I really belong here?

Was this really where I had ended up?

But almost immediately, I slipped into what I had trained myself to do for years.

I shut down.

The emotions that had burst loose just days before were sealed off again.

I went silent.

I didn't want to feel, so I watched.

The window had a narrow ledge—just wide enough for me to rest one leg on it—allowing me to lean forward and stare into the night.

Life looked different from the third floor.

The courtyard below lay in shadow, enclosed by three hospital wings forming a perfect U-shape.

The wing opposite mine drew my attention.

While most of the hospital floors were dim, a bright corner on the first floor buzzed with activity.

The rain eased, leaving the glass clear enough to reveal nurses moving swiftly, tending to rows of baby bassinets.

The maternity ward.

New beginnings.

I was on a different floor.

Not beginning anything.

Just trying not to end.

I watched until the intercom above the bathroom door shattered the quiet.

"Lights out."

Locked Doors, Locked Windows, Locked Hearts

The next morning, it blared again.

"Time to get up."

I stared at the round speaker embedded in the ceiling, shrugged, and moved without thought.

I had the room to myself—two beds, but only one occupant.

A small mercy.

Devoid of any real emotion, I showered and dressed for breakfast.

By the third day, my routine ran on autopilot.

On 3L—the psychiatric ward—everything was locked.

Locked doors.

Locked windows.

Locked hearts.

No sharp objects.

No easy escapes.

Mornings followed the same rhythm—A one-on-one with my doctor to discuss medications.

Breakfast with other patients who kept their heads down and their stories closer.

Private therapy sessions.

No friendships formed here.

Pain built walls too high for small talk to climb.

A therapist can only help when they're allowed inside the deep chasms of pain—dark places

where memories hide like shadows.

For me, those memories were locked tight, buried so deep even I could hardly reach them.

The Questions That Unraveled Me

Each morning after breakfast, I sat across from the clinical psychologist assigned to me—a kind man, soft-spoken.

That first day, we didn't talk about trauma. Not yet.

He asked why I was there. About my work. My children. How I'd been sleeping. What I'd been feeling in the weeks leading up to my admission.

It was surface-level. Just getting acquainted.

I answered politely, knowing the harder conversations were still coming—but not yet.

He was kind, and patient. But I could already feel the questions behind his questions.

The ones that waited in the shadows.
And I knew—they were coming.

The Weight of Numbness

I felt nothing.
My voice remained flat, my responses vague.
Emotion was a door I dared not open.
Numbness had become a survival tactic—a necessary armor.
I was 34 years old.
A single mother of three.
A full-time job.
To the outside world, I looked like I was holding it all together.
But I wasn't sleeping.
Food was no longer my friend.
Panic and anxiety clung to me like shadows at dusk.

The Long Road to Healing

Like grief, the trauma of sexual assault isn't something you simply recover from.
It's a journey—unpredictable, personal, slow.
It takes time to trust again.
To trust your own mind.
To trust the ground beneath your feet.
For me, it meant confronting memories I had worked so hard to bury.
Each day on 3L followed the same pattern
Locked doors.
Locked windows.
Locked hearts.

But the hardest thing to unlock wasn't made of steel or glass.

It was me.

Before I came here, I didn't know how to sit still

For years, I had filled every corner of my life with motion—raising kids, running errands, cleaning, working, jogging. When the girls were with their dad, I scrubbed the floors. If I got in the car alone, I turned on the radio before the engine even warmed. I couldn't stand the silence.

Silence meant thinking. And I couldn't afford that.

One day, right before the doctor told me I had to go to the hospital, the radio in my car quit working. I was driving alone, and I remember saying out loud, "No. Not now."

It felt like the last of my preoccupations had been stripped away.

As though life had finally cornered me—and was asking me to face what I'd spent years avoiding.

The Giving In

It was here, in this place of muted walls and scheduled meals, that I finally gave in.

Not to defeat.

But to exhaustion.

The kind of exhaustion no nap could fix.

The kind that settles in your bones, in your blood, in the silence between heartbeats.

For years, I had kept going—one foot in front of the other, smiling when I was supposed to, holding it together for everyone else.

But not here.

Here, there were no expectations to be brave.

No need to explain why my hands trembled.

Why I stared at the wall too long.

Why I couldn't finish a sandwich.

Why I had lost so much weight—not from skipping meals, but because everything I ate went straight through me.

My body wasn't absorbing nutrients.

It was done coping.

Just like I was.

Here, I was just a woman unraveling—quietly, methodically, finally.

And oddly, there was comfort in that.

Each night, I lay in the stillness of my hospital bed.

No children to tuck in.

No dishes to wash.

No overdraft charges to race.

Only silence.

And sleep.

The kind of sleep that hadn't come easily in years.

But this wasn't healing.

Not yet.

This was the quiet before the storm.

A stillness that came just before everything long buried began to surface.

There was no peace.

But there was pause.

And in its own small way—That was something.

Chapter 29
Small Beginnings

Sometimes, healing doesn't arrive with a roar.
Sometimes, it slips in quietly—like a whisper.

A flicker.

A muffin.

Healing doesn't always look like hope.

Sometimes it looks like hunger.

Sometimes it looks like something small.

On my second day, a psychiatrist began meeting with me each morning. The visits were brief, mostly focused on adjusting medications. He explained what each one was supposed to do, but I listened with only half an ear. My body was heavy with exhaustion, my thoughts slow and muddy, like trying to walk through fog.

He had started me on something new.

By day five, something shifted.

It wasn't dramatic. But it was unmistakable.

I felt hunger.

Not the hollow ache I'd grown used to—the one tangled up with dread and regret—but something gentler. I noticed a faint tug of interest at the thought of food. My stomach didn't twist in protest. My throat didn't close up with anxiety.

For so long, eating had felt like punishment. Hunger would show up, and I'd meet it with fear.

Food would follow, and pain would chase it down. The cycle was brutal and exhausting.

But something had changed.

At the hospital, meals were served past the group lounge, where patients sat quietly, shadows of themselves. We rarely spoke. That room felt like a threshold—where you remembered you weren't entirely alone, even if loneliness still clung to you like a second skin.

Beyond that room was the kitchen, where our trays waited.

For the first several days, I moved through that space like a ghost.

But on day six, everything shifted.

My sense of taste returned.

Just a little.

Just enough.

A blueberry muffin sat on my tray—soft, ordinary, forgettable by most standards. But when I took a bite, something stirred in me. The crumb clung gently to my tongue, and the blueberry burst like a quiet firework.

It was more than a taste.

It was a reminder.

It startled me—this quiet joy.

Like remembering a language I thought I'd forgotten.

Of what it felt like to enjoy something.

Of what it meant to be alive.

I chewed slowly.

Savored.

And for the first time in ages, I felt... satisfied.

Not just physically full—but filled.

A quiet contentment bloomed in my chest. Tentative. New.

At lunch, I surprised myself—I chose a hamburger. The first bite was cautious. But the flavor—the normalcy of it—made me pause. I took my time. Each mouthful felt like a tiny victory.

My body wasn't fighting me. And I, in turn, wasn't fighting life quite as hard.

At dinner, I chose lasagna and actually enjoyed it—really enjoyed it. The richness, the warmth. I let it linger in my mouth as though time didn't exist. And when dessert came—two chocolate chip cookies—I tucked them into my pocket without a second thought.

A little treasure for later.

A sweet secret I carried back to my room.

The Window and the Night

The night sky was finally clear.

A full moon hung high above the hospital, its light spilling softly through my window. It was cold. Condensation left a misty layer on the glass, a thin veil between me and the world outside.

From my small perch, I leaned in, rested one leg, and looked down into the courtyard.

The nursery caught my eye—the one connected to the maternity ward.

I unwrapped a cookie, took a bite, and let the sweetness melt on my tongue.

I watched nurses move from bassinet to bassinet, pausing gently over each swaddled bundle.

Life, brand new and unaware of its fragility, blinked in the shadows below.

I pictured the mothers, resting in nearby rooms. Smiling. Exhausted. In love.

They didn't know, I thought.

Didn't know how quickly life could break you.

Didn't know how it felt to lose yourself so completely you no longer recognized the reflection in the glass.

A heaviness settled in my chest.

Would I ever smile like that again?

The question hovered.

My breath fogged the window, softening the world into a watercolor of light and shadow.

I reached out and drew three stick figures in the condensation—simple, childish lines standing shoulder to shoulder. I added smiley faces. Crooked and hopeful.

They stared back at me—hollow, but reaching.

Fragile.

Hopeful.

A promise scribbled in fog.

Maybe I needed to see those smiles.

Even if I couldn't quite feel them yet.

I finished the last bite of the second cookie and leaned back from the window. The moon still glowed, casting silver across the bed.

I turned away.

Slipped under the covers.

It wasn't a grand transformation.

But it was something.

A muffin.

A cookie.

A smile in the glass.

Small beginnings.

And for the first time in a long while...

I let myself rest.

One breath at a time.

One small beginning at a time.

Chapter 30

When Silence Was a Weapon

I entered the hospital to heal the pieces that had shattered—but in those quiet hours on 3L, I began to understand just how long the cracks had been forming.

Before the hospital.

Before I even knew I was breaking—There was the silence.

The kind that settles into your bones and makes you forget what your own voice sounds like.

During one of my morning sessions on 3L, my counselor asked me how long I had felt this way about my marriage. My leg started bouncing. My fingers twisted into knots. I wanted to give an easy answer, but the truth pushed its way out.

"From the beginning," I said.

I met Dean when I was just eighteen. My mouth was still wired shut from the accident. I was physically healing, but emotionally? I was wrecked. I didn't understand grief yet. I didn't know that trauma doesn't fade just because time passes. I was still reeling from everything—my dad, Jonathan, my mother, my injuries, the guilt, the shame. My world had flipped upside down, and I didn't even know which way was up.

My decision was shaped by the social norms of the 1970s, where sex came after marriage—or you married the man you had already slept with. I believed it was the right thing to do once we moved in together.

Looking back from 3L, I could finally see the truth:

I wasn't ready.

Not for a relationship.

Definitely not for a marriage two years later.

Still, the marriage gave me three beautiful daughters—lives I would never take back.

Then I told the counselor about the cold dinners. How Dean wouldn't come home after work. How I'd wait and wait, no call, no explanation. Just silence. Until I'd throw the food out and tuck the girls into bed on my own.

I told him about the affair—with the wife of a couple we had called friends. When I confronted Dean, his response was casual. "I was drunk. It didn't mean anything. Doesn't matter."

But it did matter.

It humiliated me.

It hollowed out something I hadn't even realized was still whole.

I told him about the snowbank—the moment in snow country when I said the word "shit," and Dean turned toward me, eyes burning. He wasn't watching the road. We hit a snowbank. And even as the car jolted, I remember thinking, that felt good. Just saying that word. A flicker of rebellion. A glimpse of a voice I hadn't used in years.

He didn't yell.

He didn't hit.

He didn't call me names.

He just didn't speak.

And that silence drained me—day by day, year by year.

Then I told him about the card shop.

We were still living in snow country. A friend dropped me off downtown while she went to a doctor's appointment. I had Ann and Rose with me—my youngest two—Marie was in school. I stepped into my favorite stationery shop, a place I'd visited countless times for no reason at all except the comfort of soft music and pretty paper.

A girl I hadn't seen before was working the register. I smiled and reached out my hand.

"I'm Ellen Fulton," I said warmly.

Her face changed instantly. She froze—color draining from her cheeks.

Trying to fill the silence, I glanced up at the new crown molding.

"My husband remodeled this whole building," I said. "Including this shop. Isn't it beautiful?"

She hesitated. Her voice caught.

"What's your husband's name?"

I told her.

She didn't say another word.

She dropped the cards on the counter—And ran.

Straight out the back door.

And I stood there, the truth hitting me before she even cleared the threshold.

It had happened again.

Another affair. Another secret.

That afternoon, I went home, packed the girls, and left.

I never looked back.

I told the counselor that too. Told him how I'd started singing a song under my breath in the days that followed—"I'm gonna swallow my tears, harden my heart, and leave you standing here." Quarterflash. Over and over again.

It became my anthem. My armor. My goodbye.

The Call That Wasn't His to Make

After I moved out of Leah's house and was living alone, Dean kept calling—late at night, always needing something. One night, he told me he had a gun and was going to kill himself, then dropped the phone.

I panicked. I called the police. Sent them to his house.

When they arrived, he met them calmly at the door.

"Officer, I don't know what she's talking about."

That happened once.

It didn't happen again.

At least, not that way.

But the emotional manipulation?

The need to control?

That never stopped.

I used to feel like one of those plastic blow-up dolls—punched, pushed, wobbling back and forth with every hit... but somehow still upright. Still standing. Sort of.

When I entered the hospital, the staff explained the boundaries right away:

Certain people would not be allowed to visit.

Phone calls would go through the front desk, screened carefully, then—if approved—transferred to the hallway phone.

It was designed to keep patients safe.

To give us space to breathe.

But even there, he found a way in.

He had his girlfriend call the hospital pretending to be one of my friends.

The receptionist didn't know.

The call was transferred.

And I picked it up.

It was his voice.

His voice came through the phone, low and deliberate—too familiar, too controlled.

"Are you all right?" he asked. "How are you doing?"

The words might have sounded gentle to someone else, but to me, they sent a chill down my spine.

It wasn't just what he said—it was the sound of him.

That careful, practiced tone he used when he wanted to sound concerned, but still in control.

I hadn't heard his voice in weeks. On 3_, I'd been protected from it—wrapped in a cocoon of soft voices, locked doors, and a fragile sense of safety I was only just beginning to trust.

But now, that voice broke through.

It pierced the quiet I had fought so hard for, dragging me back to a place I no longer wanted to be.

My hands clenched. My stomach turned.

And without even thinking, without a single word in return—I screamed.

Not a scream of pain.

Not even of fear.

It was a scream torn from somewhere deep—raw, guttural, full of everything I hadn't been allowed to say.

It carried years of humiliation.

The affairs.

The way he'd dragged my father's friends and relatives into his bankruptcy

The silence. The distance. The endless betrayals.

All of it poured out in that one, shattering sound.

It was the sound of a boundary breaking. Of safety being stolen.

Of something inside me finally saying enough.

Later, back in my room, wrapped in a hospital blanket and the stillness that followed, the weight of it all sank in.

There was no apology. No accountability. Just that same, manipulative pity.

And something inside me snapped.

He wouldn't let me heal.

Because as long as I stayed small, ashamed, broken—He had control.

But that day, I screamed.

And I didn't apologize.

This was a time before cell phones.

No caller ID. No warnings.

The phone rang, and you picked it up.

You said hello—and hoped it wasn't someone who could unravel you.

That call didn't end my marriage.

The courts had already done that.

But it ended the part of me that still felt tethered.

Still picked up out of habit.

Still talked out of guilt.

My counselor had just told me,

"As long as you keep talking to him, you're keeping the relationship alive."

So I had started to hang up. Quietly. Without a word.

But that day, on the hallway phone—When I screamed—That was the last time.

I was done.

Done asking why.

Done wondering if I had done enough.

Done letting his sadness keep me small.

He had lost the right to my time.

My energy.

My voice.

That day, I didn't just hang up the phone.

I closed the door.

And I walked away for good.

Chapter 31
Echoes in the Hall

I had walked away from the past.

But something else was still waiting.

Today felt different.

It wasn't the weather.

It wasn't the schedule.

It was me.

In therapy, we talked about my freshman year at St. Agnes. How I'd arrived just two months after my father died. How, at fourteen, I was grieving, angry, rebellious—trying to survive. And yet somehow, I had carried the belief all these years that I was bad. That my behavior—my sarcasm, my mischief, my resistance—wasn't normal.

I remembered being pulled into the hallway for being "unladylike"— legs crossed the wrong way, chewing on a pencil during math class.

I remembered the pranks I pulled. The rules I pushed.

I thought those things defined me.

But then the therapist said something so gentle, I almost missed it.

"You were just being a normal teenager. Especially given your circumstances."

I blinked.

And then—I breathed.

It was the first time anyone had ever said that to me.

That I wasn't bad. I was just hurting.

A breath I hadn't known I'd been holding for years left my body like steam rising off pavement.

Something loosened in me. As if that one sentence had gently closed a silent chapter I didn't realize was still open.

I nodded slowly and whispered, "Thank you."

We talked about how much I missed my friends while I was away at school.

How hard it was to reconnect with them on the weekends—like we were on opposite sides of a river I didn't know how to cross.

Something in me had always felt left behind.

And now, somehow... something inside me was catching up. Gently, but undeniably.

The Sounds in the Night

That night, I lay in bed staring at the ceiling, replaying the conversation.

There was no therapy scheduled today, but still—something had shifted.

Was it good?

I wasn't sure.

That uncertainty hovered around me like a question that hadn't found its answer yet.

I couldn't shake the feeling that something big was coming. Something I had almost let myself forget.

I got up and walked to the window, the cold floor biting against my bare feet.

Outside, the maternity ward's drapes were drawn. The light I had looked for so many nights before—gone. The nursery quiet.

The night sky stretched black and endless.

Still.

I pressed my palm to the glass, feeling its coolness seep into my skin. Something inside me felt equally still—like I was waiting for something I couldn't name.

Monday's session was already on my mind.

There was something waiting for me there.

Something I had carried so long it had become part of my bones.

Something I hadn't looked at yet.

A cold knot twisted in my stomach, but underneath it... something warmer. A flicker of hope.

I wasn't sure what I was reaching for.

But I knew I was getting closer.

I stepped back, climbed into bed, and pulled the blanket up to my chin.

The scent of clean linen—a trace of bleach and something softer—filled the space around me.

Familiar. Safe.

But then—Footsteps.

Fast. Heavy.

And then—Screaming.

Shrill. Panicked.

I froze.

Pam.

I had just sat with her at lunch earlier in the week. Tuesday, then again Wednesday.

Now, her voice ripped through the hallway like a jagged tear in the stillness.

It wasn't the first time.

The night before—Thursday—she had screamed too.

But this?

This was worse.

Raw.

Desperate.

Her voice didn't just echo.

It tore.

Through the hallway.

Through the night.

Through me.

I lay in bed, clutching my blanket, heart racing.

What had happened to her?

What was she remembering?

What had broken loose inside her?

I didn't want to think about it.

But I couldn't stop hearing her cries.

They clung to the ceiling. The walls. My thoughts.

Tomorrow was Saturday.

Arts and crafts in the afternoon.

I hoped to see her there.

We hadn't spoken much. But something about her stayed with me.

And now, after the screaming... even more so.

There was something about Pam I couldn't explain.

Maybe because somewhere, just beneath the surface—My own scream was waiting too.

And I was starting to hear it.

Chapter 32
The Art of
Surviving

Snip. Snip. Snip.

The rhythmic sound of scissors slicing through construction paper filled the room, blending with the soft rustle of magazine pages turning and the occasional scrape of a glue stick against cardboard.

The sound was strangely soothing—like stitching something broken, one cut at a time. The sharp scent of paper, glue, and disinfectant hung in the air—a strange mixture of childhood nostalgia and hospital sterility.

It was Saturday—Arts and Crafts Day—on the fourth floor, known to all of us simply as 4L.

Arts and Crafts Day was meant for expression—a way to release emotions too tangled for words.

My therapist had suggested it might help me regain focus, maybe even create something out of the chaos I'd unraveled during yesterday's session.

We hadn't talked about the worst things yet—not the ones buried furthest down. Yesterday had been about St. Agnes. About arriving just two months after my dad died. About how I wasn't bad—I was grieving. Fourteen. Lost. Acting out in ways that were completely understandable.

Human.

Still, it had left me raw. Unsteady.

And now, I was being asked to cut and paste—literally—as if assembling something whole out of scraps could somehow translate to healing.

Four of us from 3L were cleared to go. Pam was one of them.

When we stepped into the elevator, I felt her presence before I even looked at her.

She was there, but only barely—like a shadow clinging to itself.

She was small and petite, with pale blond hair that looked like it hadn't been brushed in days.

Her shoulders seemed to fold in on themselves, like she was trying to disappear. I remembered her being sharp-witted, even funny, earlier in the week—but now, that girl was gone.

She stood quietly in the corner, her arms wrapped around herself, eyes locked on the buttons above the doors.

She hadn't spoken since we left the lounge. Just... silence.

It was the first time I'd seen her since the screaming.

Two nights in a row, her voice had sliced through the stillness of 3L— first with raw panic, then something deeper, darker.

And now, she was here—quiet. Small. Present, but distant.

Her eyes didn't meet mine.

The elevator doors opened with a hiss, revealing a hallway that felt more like a holding place than a healing one.

The walls were narrower. Dimmer. The overhead lights buzzed faintly, casting a dull, uneven glow over the floor.

The windows were high and thin—no view of the outside world, only hints of daylight seeping in at strange angles.

There were cameras in the corners. And doors that locked from the outside.

Ben, the therapist leading the session, walked with us down the hallway. As we entered the arts and crafts room, he gave us a quick glance, then turned back to the door.

Click.

He locked it behind us.

That sound—the click of the lock—echoed louder in my chest than I expected. It reminded me how thin the line was between being a patient and being protected from yourself.

This was 4L.

The patients here weren't allowed around anything sharp. No scissors. No pencils. Not even paper clips.

But we—visitors from 3L—were trusted to use them.

It hit me in a strange way. Not pride, exactly. But awareness.

We were led into a large activity room where a long table stretched across the space, surrounded by metal chairs that screeched against the tile floor.

Ben smiled as he slid colorful bins onto the table. "Pick anything that speaks to you," he said gently.

Scissors, glue sticks, old magazines, construction paper. Everything colorful, tactile, and meant to help us create something.

To my surprise, I was drawn to the collage bin.

I picked a theme: fashion and flowers.

There was something rhythmic in it—the snipping, the arranging. Maybe I just needed something I could control.

Snip. Snip.

I worked slowly, choosing bold silhouettes and vibrant blooms. But even as my hands moved, part of me stayed aware of the girl sitting across from me.

Pam.

She hadn't touched a thing.

She sat with her hands in her lap, her shoulders hunched slightly forward, eyes staring down at the table.

There was no trace of the girl I'd seen earlier in the week, the one who could toss out sarcastic remarks or crack a crooked smile.

Only this version—silent, slumped, her entire body weighted by something invisible.

I leaned over and gently asked, "Are you okay?"

She hesitated, then said softly, "I made the call this morning."

I didn't know what she meant, but something about the way she said it made me pause.

"My therapist said I needed to tell my mom... about what my stepfather used to do."

She didn't look up.

"When I was younger. The horrible things." Her voice was flat, too exhausted to carry emotion.

"And I told her everything."

She finally looked at me.

Pam was 28 years old. And in that moment, she looked like a child who had just lost everything.

"She said I was a liar. That I was trying to destroy her marriage. Then she told me I was no longer welcome in her home."

Her mouth trembled. "Then she hung up."

The world didn't break apart.

But Pam did.

I reached out without thinking and placed my hand over hers.

She didn't cry. She didn't scream. She just stared—silent, stunned, and devastated.

Her voice had kept me awake the last two nights. But this quiet—this aching stillness—was worse.

The longer I sat, the more my project began to blur.

The fashion spreads. The flowers. The careful cutting. It all felt meaningless.

The act of arranging fragments into something beautiful suddenly felt too familiar.

Wasn't that what I'd been doing with myself all along?

Trying to gather the pieces.

Cutting away the damage.

Rearranging the parts.

Hoping to create something I could recognize—something that felt whole, even if it wasn't.

How hard it is to gather the pieces when you're still bleeding from the breaks.

How easy it is to pretend the cuts have closed when they're still weeping underneath.

Across from me, Pam sat still, her eyes fixed on nothing, her hands unmoving in her lap.

And somehow, sitting there in that quiet, locked room—surrounded by scraps of paper and the weight of everything unsaid—I realized how fragile it all was.

Later that afternoon, back on 3L, I was sitting in the lounge when the intercom crackled overhead.

"Telephone call for Lennie." The nurse gestured toward the hallway phone.

It was my sister. She asked if I wanted to go to lunch the next day—Sunday.

It would be the first time in over a week that I'd been outside the hospital.

That morning, my doctor had told me I was stable enough to leave for a few hours with approved family members.

In therapy, I had shared that I felt safe with my oldest sister and her husband.

Still, I had mixed feelings. What would we talk about? Would I feel like myself—or like someone they were tiptoeing around?

Part of me wanted to say no. To stay wrapped in the strange safety of routine.

But another part—the one that had sat across from Pam and witnessed what it meant to speak the truth—knew I needed to go.

That night, I curled up by the window.

It had become my place. My spot to breathe. To think. To try to feel something other than numb.

Only this time, I didn't stare across the courtyard toward the maternity ward.

I looked up—into the dark, endless sky.

Tomorrow was Sunday. And for a few short hours, I would be stepping outside.

Not just outside the hospital, but outside the version of me that believed I was broken beyond repair.

Maybe that's what healing really was.

Not perfection.

Just the slow, steady act of gathering the pieces—

one breath,

one truth,

one day at a time.

Chapter 33
Stepping Outside

The next morning, the smell of coffee drifted through the hallways. The scent clung to the air—like hope.

Or a memory you're not sure you can trust.

As I passed the reception station, a nurse called out to me.

"You had a call earlier this morning reminding us you have a lunch date today."

I smiled. "Thank you. It will be nice to be outside again," I said, the words hesitant on my tongue.

Would it?

I wasn't sure.

I wasn't sure I was ready to hear any voice from the outside world.

I wasn't sure I was ready to be reminded of the person I was before I walked through these doors.

The doors leading out of 3L, a firm reminder that leaving wasn't something you could just decide to do.

A staff member approached with a set of keys. The metallic jingle echoed in the quiet hallway, louder than it should have been.

With a turn of the lock, the door clicked open.

And just like that, the world unfolded before me.

A world too bright.

Too loud.

Too real.

I hesitated.

Was my mind ready?

The world beyond those doors felt distant. Disorienting.

It had only been two weeks, but inside 3L, time moved differently—slower, softer, more structured.

My breath caught, just for a moment. The hesitation held me in place.

Then, with a quiet exhale, I forced my feet forward.

My sister Alice and brother-in-law George were waiting to take me out for lunch.

They knew this would be my first step outside the walls of the hospital, and they had chosen a small restaurant across the street.

Something manageable.

Something that wouldn't swallow me whole.

As we crossed the street, I glanced at Alice—steady, composed, the way she had always been.

In that moment, I realized she reminded me of the porcelain doll I had loved so much as a child.

Small, delicate features. Blonde hair.

My sister was beautiful—inside and out.

I thought of her bedroom when I was five—how I'd quietly step past the giant stuffed animals her boyfriends had won at the fair, just to stand inches from that doll.

Back then, I tiptoed into her world in awe.

Now, it was her gently stepping into mine.

Years earlier, after the accident that killed Mom and Jonathan, Alice and George had taken me in—tried to give me a home. Even though I felt out of place, they did everything they could to make me comfortable.

Alice never let me see her grief, but I know now how much she must have been carrying. Mom had been her best friend.

Still, she picked me up from the hospital back then.

She showed up.

Just like she was showing up now.

Back then, I couldn't feel the depth of what they were offering me. I was too numb.

But now, years later, sitting beside her at that quiet restaurant, I was finally starting to feel the feelings I couldn't access back then.

The air hit my skin in an unexpected way—cool, crisp... foreign.

It wasn't just the temperature.

It was the openness. The noise. The lack of walls to lean against.

A bus pulled away from the curb just down the block. Its brakes hissed, and the sound snapped through me like static.

A woman's laughter echoed off a nearby wall—too loud, too sudden. I flinched before I could stop myself.

For a moment, I felt like the space around me was too wide, like I could fall into it and not be found.

I had longed for this moment, but now that it was here, part of me wanted to retreat.

The restaurant was warm and quiet. Soft lighting. Low chatter. The clink of silverware against ceramic.

It should have felt normal.

But everything felt slightly out of sync, like I was moving through someone else's life.

Alice and George didn't push. They didn't ask how I was feeling or what therapy had uncovered.

Instead, we talked lightly—about the weather, a new store Alice had visited, how George had burned the toast that morning.

It was easy. It was light.

And yet I felt like I was watching it all from a distance, like I was just a shadow at the table.

A ghost trying to learn how to eat among the living.

I used to be good at this.

Ordering lunch. Making conversation.

Laughing at stories that didn't have trauma threaded through them.

Now, even choosing a drink felt like a small test.

Even smiling felt like effort.

The world was still spinning, but I was just learning how to stand.

After lunch, we stood on the sidewalk.

The hospital stood just across the street, unmoving. Waiting. I let out a slow breath.

"You ready to go back?" George asked gently.

I nodded.

I was.

Inside, the routines made sense. The quiet was predictable. I didn't have to explain myself.

In 3L, no one expected me to be okay.

Inside, brokenness wasn't shameful.

It was understood.

As I stepped toward the building, I realized something unexpected.

I was relieved to go back.

The outside world—open, unfiltered, unfinished—was still too much.

But 3L had become a kind of sanctuary.

A place where the healing had begun.

As I reached the door, I turned and looked back over my shoulder.

The world was still there.

Waiting.

And maybe—one day—I'd be ready for it.

But not today.

Today, I was still gathering the pieces.

And that was enough.

Chapter 34
Giving It a Name

It was toward the end of the week when it happened.

I walked into the therapy session carrying something I didn't even realize was still buried.

Carrying it so long it had become part of me—invisible, but heavy.

Pam had been on my mind all week.

The sound of her screaming through the halls—first on Thursday, then again Friday—had stayed with me. Even in the quietest moments, her voice echoed inside me. The pain she had released into the air had stirred something I hadn't been ready to name.

Pam had broken open in front of me.

And somehow, that gave me permission to crack too.

Maybe part of me had started to wonder what it would feel like to speak the truth out loud.

There was no agenda—no specific topic I planned to bring up.

Just me, the familiar chair across from him, and that unspoken heaviness that had followed me for years.

I sat down, but I didn't settle.

He asked me something—I don't remember what—but suddenly I was staring past him, my focus drifting to a blank spot on the wall.

The book-lined room looked different somehow. Warmer, but distant.

Like I had stepped into a memory rather than a moment.

My eyes kept scanning the spines, searching for something—words, maybe—that didn't yet exist in my mouth.

I took a step back.

Not physically, but emotionally. Internally.

I could feel myself go into that space.

Detached. Silent. On the edge of something I'd spent years avoiding.

I was holding a warm cup of coffee, something I had brought with me like a comfort object—solid, familiar, grounding.

But my fingers were trembling.

When I finally set it down, I nearly missed the coffee table.

That's how far gone I was.

I wasn't fully in the room anymore.

My chest tightened.

I couldn't catch a full breath.

I didn't even know what was coming until it was already there.

And then—without warning—I heard myself say it.

"I was a virgin."

The words barely made it out.

They floated there—fragile and heavy—before falling into the space between us.

My voice caught in my throat, trembling under the weight of what came next.

"My pregnancy... it came from that."

The room went still.

My mind went numb immediately.

It was the only safe place I knew how to go.

My therapist, a kind-eyed man with a gentle presence, didn't rush me.

He didn't interrupt.

He just sat with me in that stillness.

I looked down at my hands.

They were shaking slightly, resting on my knees, palms up—like I was holding something fragile and broken.

Tears welled up, but I didn't cry right away.

I was still somewhere else—half in the room, half trapped in a moment I had never given voice to.

"I've never said that out loud before," I whispered.

He stayed quiet. Not shocked. Just present.

And then, after a few moments, he said softly:

"You did not deserve that."

I nodded, too. Slowly.

It wasn't just that I kept it secret.

I had carried the shame like it was mine.

But it wasn't mine.

And saying it—finally—was the first time I felt that.

The ache moved through me slowly, catching in my chest, tightening around my ribs.

I wanted to run.

I wanted to vanish.

But I didn't.

I stayed.

I had said the words.

And in doing so, I had reclaimed a piece of myself.

I stood up slowly, my legs unsteady.

Then I walked back to my room.

The hallway felt quiet, as if the walls were giving me space to breathe.

That Night at the Window

That night, I sat at the window and let my thoughts drift into the blackness outside.

I didn't cry.

I just stared, quiet, unsure of what had just happened to me.

I had spoken the truth for the first time—and the weight of it was still settling inside me.

And yet, somewhere beneath the ache, I felt something else.

Safe.

I knew it now—3L had become that for me.

Not because it erased the pain, but because it finally gave me space to feel it.

After a while, I shifted my gaze toward the nursery.

Its soft light glowed faintly in the distance.

It used to draw me in with the promise of new life—something pure, untouched.

Tonight, it felt different.

I wasn't looking for rebirth.

I was honoring something quieter.

The moment I gave my pain a name—and didn't turn away.

Chapter 35
The Girl on the Hill

It was Monday, and I was exhausted.

The air felt thicker somehow—as if even breathing took effort.

All weekend, I had felt drained—like my body was still processing the weight of everything that had surfaced the week before.

I walked into my therapist's office, dropped into the chair, and wrapped my fingers around the cup of coffee I hadn't yet sipped from.

He waited a moment, then asked gently, "What's coming up for you today?"

I stared at the cup. "I've been thinking about the girl and the accident again."

He nodded. "The one you've described before—the image of the girl climbing?"

"Yes." I paused. "I kept seeing her. Climbing, climbing, climbing up the side of the embankment."

My voice dropped. "I think... I just realized something."

He leaned forward, quietly present. "Tell me."

"That girl," I said, staring at the floor. "It was me."

And I had left her there.

The room went still.

"I didn't realize it until now—until being here on 3L, where everything's been slowed down and I've finally been looking at the past."

I paused. "She was wearing the same brown suede coat I had. Same jeans. Same hair."

My eyes filled, but I didn't look away.

"She was climbing the hill alone, slipping, shaking. Blood on her hands. I kept seeing it, like a movie I couldn't turn off."

He nodded, gently. "And now you know that memory wasn't of someone else."

I inhaled shakily. "No. It was me. I was watching myself."

And I had left her there for so long.

Alone.

Bleeding.

Climbing.

He let the silence stretch.

I looked at him, my voice quieter now. "The next thing I remember... I was beating on the chest of an ambulance driver."

His expression didn't change, but I felt the weight of his presence.

"He wouldn't go down the hill. Wouldn't go back to help."

I swallowed. "My baby. My mom. They were still down there. And he wouldn't move."

"Do you remember what you said?" he asked.

"I don't remember saying anything. Just pounding on his chest. I must've been screaming, but I don't remember hearing myself. Just the rage. The panic."

Pounding.

Screaming without sound.

Begging.

And nothing—no one—moved.

Like if I hit hard enough, I could make time reverse.

I hesitated, then added, "My jaw was broken."

He looked up at me. "You were injured and didn't even know."

I shook my head. "Didn't feel it. All I could think about was getting them out. I just kept hitting him, I must have been begging him to go."

We sat in that quiet space for a while, both of us holding it.

"I've carried that image for so long," I whispered. "This girl climbing and climbing, and I never saw her face."

"And now?"

"I see her clearly. She's me."

My voice cracked.

"She was trying to survive. Trying to get help. With everything broken, she was still climbing."

He leaned back slightly, nodding again. "And maybe now, you don't have to climb alone."

I didn't answer. Just breathed.

And for the first time since the image began replaying in my mind, I stopped watching her from a distance.

I reached for her.

And maybe—for the first time—she reached back.

That Night

I don't remember much from the day of the accident.

My brain has protected me for years from the full impact of what happened that day.

But one image has returned to me again and again: the girl on the embankment.

Climbing, slipping, shaking.

I thought she was someone else.

Now I know—she was me.

That realization didn't break me.

It brought me back to myself.

And for the first time, I wasn't watching from a distance.

I reached for her.

And maybe—for the first time—she reached back.

That night, I stood at the window in my room.

The glass was cool beneath my fingertips, the hallway quiet behind me.

I didn't cry. I didn't scream.

I just looked out, steady and still—knowing that for the first time, I wasn't looking for her.

I was standing with her.

Chapter 36
The Pieces I Carried

It was Tuesday morning, and everything felt a little softer. Like dust settling after a storm.

Not lighter. Not easier.

But quieter.

I don't remember how I slept that night. Some part of me must have—my body needed it—but my mind felt like it had been cracked open and rearranged.

I stayed in bed longer than usual. The familiar buzz of morning routines on 3L drifted in through the hallway—footsteps, coffee, soft voices. But I didn't move right away.

I just lay there, letting the stillness settle over me.

I thought about everything I had uncovered in the past week. About Pam's screams, and the pain that lived underneath them. About the words I had spoken in the therapist's office—the ones I had never said out loud. About the girl in the brown suede coat, clawing her way up the side of a hill while the rest of her world crumbled below.

She had been with me all this time.

Not just in memories, but in the way I flinched when things got too quiet.

In the way I kept myself busy so I wouldn't feel.

In the way I tried to save everyone else, while quietly sinking myself.

I had carried her pain in pieces.

Until now.

Now, the pieces had names.

Now, the grief had edges.

Sharp enough to touch.

Sharp enough to name.

Now, the memory had a face.

Mine.

There was something strange about recognizing yourself in a memory you had always kept at a distance. It changed everything. Made it real. Made it yours.

I had always told myself I was strong for surviving.

But that morning, I realized something else.

I was also strong for remembering.

Strong for slowing down.

Strong for staying long enough to look at what hurt.

I finally rose and made my way to the window—the one I always returned to when the weight in my chest needed somewhere to go.

Outside, the sky was pale and overcast. Still waking up.

I watched the light stretch across the courtyard. The wind moved through the trees in soft waves, as if the earth itself knew how heavy healing could be.

I wrapped my arms around myself and breathed with it.

Not in defiance.

But in acknowledgment.

And without even thinking, I started to hum.

Sometimes I feel like a motherless child...

Soft. Barely audible.

But the ache of it vibrated in my chest.

I hadn't realized how long I'd been carrying that feeling.

I had lived through things that no one should ever have to live through.

And I was still here.

Still waking.

Still climbing.

Still gathering the pieces.

Chapter 37
Where The Grief Lived

The day after I hummed "Sometimes I Feel Like a Motherless Child," the sound stayed with me.

Soft. Worn. True.

It clung to me like breath—whispered through each step, each blink, each ache.

Wednesday came.

I sat across from my therapist in that small room, the one with the soft lamp and tissue box always within reach. We began to talk—about the accident. About my mom. About Jonathan.

And then, after a long silence, he asked softly,

"Is there a part of this that still lives in you, but you've never put into words?"

That's when my body betrayed me.

My hands—without warning—began to curl inward. First one finger, then another. The joints twisted, tight and slow, until both hands looked arthritic. Bent. Clawed. Frozen.

My breathing changed—shallow, quick. A tightness gripped my stomach, sharp and unforgiving Pain surged through the soles of my feet, sudden and electric, as if my body had been struck from the inside out.

I stared at my hands, stunned. My therapist paused.

I couldn't keep talking about them. Not yet.

I closed my eyes, trying to remember—to see their faces. But instead, what I saw was my heart.

Not the shape of it, not a medical diagram.

But the feeling of it.

I saw it splinter—fracturing into countless tiny pieces.

And then I saw those pieces fall.

Down.

Down.

To the floor.

They hit the tile like porcelain.

Bright red. Scattered like glass. Like grief. Like everything I had tried so hard to hold.

That's when the silent screams began.

My mouth opened wide, my head tilted back, reaching for something—air, God, escape.

But no sound came out.

Just the raw, aching stretch of a scream that had lived inside me for years.

I felt it surge through my body—like a current.

From the soles of my feet to the crown of my head, it ripped through me.

I hugged myself so tightly, as if I could hold all the pieces together by sheer force.

But something had broken open.

Something I hadn't even known was locked away.

And in the middle of that storm—one clear thought broke through the chaos:

I just want them back.

I want my mom and Jonathan alive.

Here.

With me.

I missed them so much my whole body hurt with it.

It wasn't just sadness. It was longing. Bone-deep, soul-deep longing.

The kind that makes you forget where you are.

The kind that floods every cell with ache.

The room felt cold—unnaturally cold.

Not the kind of cold that came from a thermostat, but a bone-deep chill that settled into my skin and made my arms tremble.

The soft lamplight flickered slightly, casting shadows on the walls.

Pain came in waves—raw, searing.

Not just emotional. Not just physical. It was both.

A crushing tightness took hold of my chest, like a fist pressing inward, stealing air.

I couldn't breathe deeply, couldn't swallow.

My fingers, still bent and twisted at the joints, felt like claws wrapped around grief itself.

I had never felt so exposed. So cracked open.

I was afraid if I moved, I would shatter.

My therapist didn't rush in with questions. He didn't try to fix it or name it.

He just sat there—in silence—letting me feel it.

Letting me cry.

And I did.

Big, heavy sobs that came from somewhere deep.

Deeper than I even knew I had.

All the while, my hands stayed knotted and curled.

But as I cried, something began to shift.

Slowly, gradually, my fingers started to loosen.

The tightness began to ease.

The ache retreated.

By the time the tears had slowed, my hands had returned to normal.

The longing remained—but softer now. Quieter.

Still there, but no longer screaming.

He still didn't speak.

Not until I was ready.

And then, gently, he said, "We're not going to go any further with this today."

He paused, thoughtful. Then he offered an image—one I would carry with me for years.

"Your past is like a ball of yarn," he said. "Wound up tight, but with little ends starting to stick out all over. Each one leads to something important. Something you'll need to explore over time."

He looked at me with calm certainty.

"But not this one. Not yet."

I would later learn it might've been something called a somatic flashback—a way trauma speaks when words won't come.

He didn't explain what had happened. Didn't give it a label.

And I didn't ask.

Was it a memory trying to surface?

Was my body remembering something my mind could not?

To this day, I still don't know.

All I remember is the smell of burning rubber.

And a girl—climbing the embankment.

Everything else is gone.

Like smoke.

Like a closed door I'm not sure ever needs to be opened.

The cold lingered. Not from the room, but from what had almost broken through.

And somewhere inside me, the music still played—soft and low.

Sometimes I feel like a motherless child.

Only now, I didn't hum it.

I felt it.

Chapter 38
Jonathan Was Here

I was still tired from the week before—emotionally spent—but something inside me stirred when I heard the nurse call out:"You have a call.". The hum of hospital life surrounded me. Filing drawers opened and closed. The click of a stapler, the clack of a keyboard, the rustle of papers blended into the background noise, mingling with the comforting aroma of fresh coffee wafting through the air.

I glanced at the stark pale green walls that had been my home for almost 4 weeks. Clean. Sterile. Impersonal. No artwork. No decorations. Just one lone black patient phone, bolted to the wall. "You have a call. From your brother, Arthur," the nurse said, smiling. "We told him to try back at 8:00 a.m." I thanked her, feeling something unexpected—excitement.

It had been a while since I had felt genuinely happy to talk to someone from the outside. I could hear the buzz of hospital activity as I walked down the hallway toward the patient phone hanging on the wall. Someone else was using it.

I kept a respectful distance, waiting, my hands folded in front of me, my slippers shuffling slightly against the floor.

The harsh fluorescent lights above flickered slightly, their cold, artificial glow making me long for the warmth of the outdoors.

Finally, the phone was available.I took a deep breath, hoping hoping my brother was coming to see me. He was tomorrow afternoon.

Reconnecting with My Brother

When Arthur arrived, he looked the exact same as one year ago.

He wore a subtle tie-dye t-shirt, muted blues, yellows, and purples peeking out beneath his denim bib overalls His classic look. My oldest brother. Always.

I met him in the downstairs lobby, surprisingly navigating the hospital by myself.

He had moved back from California years ago and now lived in our hometown—the same small town where we had grown up.

For years he had been the activity director of our local historical society, serving as vice president for a time. Before that, when we were kids, he had been the town's paperboy, the kind that rode his bike and tossed newspapers onto porches in the early morning light.

And now here he stood, grinning, his eyes twinkling like they always had.

He looked like farmer Joe, standing there in his overalls, but he had the same gentle, happy presence I had always known. Our eyes met, and we both smiled. It felt good to see him.

He pulled me into a big, warm hug, holding me tightly "How are you doing, sis?" he whispered. He smelled of sweet musk, a familiar scent that instantly grounded me.

The warmth of his embrace was overwhelming. I had been dealing with so much emotion on my own that I had forgotten what a good hug felt like—comforting, welcoming, real.

I exhaled deeply, letting myself sink into the familiarity of my brother's presence.

"I'm doing okay," I replied, looking up at him.

I knew he genuinely cared.

I also knew that everything I had been going through—this hospital stay, the therapy, the memories resurfacing—would be foreign to him.

We kept our conversation light. He asked about my girls, and I told him I had just spoken to them the day before. Then, Arthur suggested something unexpected.

"Let's not go to a restaurant. Let's take a walk instead." I hesitated for only a moment before nodding.

"Okay," I agreed. I felt closer to him in that moment than I had in years.

He understood that I was going through something difficult— otherwise, I wouldn't be here.

And he didn't need to talk about it to acknowledge it.

A Walk Through the City

The fresh air outside was crisp against my face.

The naked branches of the deciduous trees stood stark against the clear blue sky, their silhouettes like giant spokes reaching toward the heavens.

It was almost as though I were seeing and hearing the world differently, more acutely.

The way the cold air filled my lungs, the way my footsteps echoed slightly against the pavement—everything felt more real.

I looked over at my brother. We walked in comfortable silence.

I wasn't sure if I had changed, or if the world had.

Arthur motioned toward a park bench, and I nodded.

We sat down.

The chill of the metal seeped through my jacket, sending a shiver through me.

We watched the hustle and bustle of the big city unfold before us.

People bundled up in winter coats hurried past.

Random voices mixed in the air—conversations half-heard, fragments of other people's lives.

A horn honked in the distance.

The low, grinding noise of a bulldozer rumbled somewhere down the street.

Life was moving forward.

And I was still here.

Another day.

Sitting across from my brother, who I loved very much.

"Arthur, you went to Mom and Jonathan's funeral."

The words came out calmly, without hesitation.

"What was it like? I was in the hospital and didn't go."

Arthur sighed, looking off into the distance as he recalled that day.

"That's right, sis. I had forgotten you didn't attend it. I suppose it was like most funerals. A lot of people were there," he said, remembering.

Then, he paused for a moment before continuing.

"Mom and your son were in the same casket. Jonathan was laid beside Mom."

His hand pressed gently over mine as he spoke.

We sat in silence for a few moments after he told me about the funeral—how Jonathan had been laid beside of Mom in the casket. The image settled heavy in my chest, but I didn't look away from it. I let it be there. I let myself feel it.

Then Arthur shifted slightly beside me, like he had more to say.

"Sis..." he began gently, "I'm almost positive little Jonathan was brought to this hospital after the accident."

I looked at him, startled.

"This hospital? Here?"

He nodded. "Yeah. I've thought about it ever since you told me where you were staying. I remember someone saying it back then—this was the closest trauma center. And that's where they brought him first."

My heart slowed.

My breath caught in my throat.

Jonathan.

Here.

These same hallways.

These same walls.

Maybe not 3L. But somewhere.

I stared ahead, struggling to speak.

"Do you know for sure?" I finally asked, turning my head to stare at the hospital.

Arthur gave a small shrug. "I don't. Not yet. But I think George would remember. He was involved with all the logistics back then. I'll ask him, and I'll let you know."

I nodded slowly.

"Okay," I whispered.

The wind stirred around us, brushing through the trees, but neither of us moved.

Arthur reached over and gave my hand a gentle squeeze.

"He could have been here, sis. And now... so are you."

I felt his words before I fully processed them.

My chest tightened.

Tears spilled down my cheeks before I even realized I was crying.

Imagining them together like that... together. For the first time.

And I hadn't known.

How did I not know.

How did no one tell me.

The questions echoed through my head, sharp and relentless.

And then—another thought hit me.

Back then, I'd been in a hospital bed with a fractured jaw. I was on so much morphine I could barely stay awake. I'd vomited from the pain. Dry heaves tore through me during withdrawal.

My mind had been in a fog I couldn't climb out of.

Maybe someone did tell me.

I just couldn't remember.

That realization sank into me differently. Not like guilt. Not like blame. Just... sorrow.

What else had I missed while I was floating between pain and oblivion.

I closed my eyes.

And for a moment, I felt something shift.

Not in the air.

In me.

A quiet presence.

A warmth I hadn't felt in years.

Not memory.

Not imagination.

Just a simple, overwhelming knowing.

Jonathan was here.

The silence stretched between Arthur and me, heavy with everything said and unsaid.

Chapter 39
He Was Never Lost

I woke up with a strange mix of fatigue and urgency.

The previous day had unraveled me.

I had stood at the window, pressing my hands to the glass, grappling with the realization that Jonathan might have been here.

I had spent the night tossing, my mind replaying the same haunting image—Me, kneeling, picking up the shattered pieces of my heart.

Now, I had to carry them into daylight.

I didn't know it yet, but today would hand me another piece—one I wasn't ready for.

I skipped breakfast and walked to the kitchen area to pour a cup of coffee, waiting impatiently for my brother's call.

It finally came.

He confirmed it—Jonathan had been taken to this hospital after the accident.

I barely registered the familiar faces murmuring their morning greetings.

I nodded vaguely, my gray sweatpants and moccasin slippers reflecting how quickly I had dressed.

The only thing that mattered now was what I needed to do next.

Meet with my therapist and tell him what I had just learned.

The Therapist's Call

I entered the therapy room, the scent of aged books and something vaguely herbal filling the air.

The walls—lined with bookshelves, worn leather chairs, and quiet understanding—had become familiar.

But today, everything felt different.

I sat down, gripping my coffee cup tightly.

I needed to tell him. Why, I wasn't sure—but he had become my confidant. Maybe the hospital had records?

"Good morning, Ellen."

I could barely get the words out fast enough.

"I met with my brother yesterday. He told me that Jonathan was brought to this hospital after the accident. Do you think the hospital keeps records that far back—from 1971?"

"Not likely," he said gently. "They usually only keep them for ten years."

I slumped in my chair.

"Let me make a call after our session today," he added. "I'll let you know what I find out."

He didn't sound hopeful.

But still—he thought it was worth looking.

Waiting in my room afterward was the hardest part.

If there were records... somehow it meant I'd know where my son spent the final days of his short life. Maybe I'd learn how he died.

I'd know he was really gone.

Without realizing it, I had carried this quiet belief that maybe—just maybe—he hadn't died. That I would find him alive one day.

Silly thoughts, maybe.

But deep grief lets you play with those kinds of stories.

At exactly 2:00 p.m., there was a knock on my door.

My heart pounded as I listened to my therapist's voice, calm and steady.

"There's a chance—a small one—that the files still exist. I think it's worth taking a look. They'd be in the basement."

His words settled into my chest, hope and fear mixing in equal parts.

Then came the question.

"Does that sound like somewhere you'd like to go? Tomorrow—Saturday—would be the best day."

I took a breath.

And then, quietly, with certainty, I said:

"Yes."

Descending Into the Past

The hallway felt longer than usual as we walked toward the elevator.

Each step was heavier, like I was walking toward something I wasn't sure I was ready for.

The ding of the elevator broke the silence.

I watched the numbers count down—3... 2...

I clenched my hands into fists at my sides.

1... B.

The elevator stopped, and the doors slid open.

The air changed immediately—cooler, heavier, carrying the scent of dust and aging paper.

Dim overhead lights cast long shadows, making the rows of metal shelves look endless.

The silence here was different—waiting.

Waiting for someone to remember.

Waiting for someone to search.

We started looking—my therapist and I—pulling down box after box. File after file.

Nothing.

Minutes stretched into what felt like hours.

My hope began to fade, slipping through my fingers like sand.

My therapist sighed, closing another box.

"It's not looking promising," he said gently. "I'm sorry we weren't able to find any records dated back that far."

He reached for the light switch.

That's when I saw it.

A dusty, worn box, sitting high on a shelf right above me, tucked into a corner.

I pointed up, my voice barely above a whisper.

"What about that one?"

My voice barely broke the heavy silence.

But somehow, I knew.

He followed my gaze, hesitated, then nodded.

We reached for it, brushing off the thick layer of dust.

The lid creaked open.

Inside—old medical records, files with papers yellowed by time.

And then—There.

His name.

Jonathan Guiles

My breath caught.

After all these years, after all the silence, after all the running—Jonathan had been here all along.

The Words That Broke Me

I opened the file, my hands trembling as I pulled back the yellowed pages inside.

My eyes scanned the paper, desperately searching for his name—for any sign of him.

At first, the words blurred together, the letters difficult to focus on—as if my brain was refusing to process what was in front of me.

But then—There.

Jonathan.

The day they admitted him.

How long he lived.

How he died.

My breath hitched, my chest tightening, as my fingers traced the printed sentences.

Trauma to his head.

Complications of brain swelling and bleeding.

The words sat starkly on the page—final, definitive, permanent.

Tears spilled down my cheeks, falling onto the fragile pages.

I had spent so long avoiding this moment.

Now, there was no avoiding it.

For years, I had daydreamed about finding him alive.

I had allowed myself to believe in an impossible hope.

But the file in my hands told me the truth.

He had never left this hospital.

He had never left my mother's side.

And I had never asked until now.

Jonathan was real.

Jonathan was here.

Jonathan was gone.

And so was the last fragile hope I had clung to.

Closing the File & Leaving the Past Where It Was Found

I didn't want to close the file.

Not yet.

As long as it was open in front of me, he felt close.

But there was nothing left to learn.

Only what had already been written. Recorded. Stored away.

My therapist stood quietly nearby, watching.

Then he gently said, "I'll give you a few moments."

I nodded as he stepped out of the records room, leaving me alone with the file.

The tears came freely.

There was no one to hide them from.

I don't know how long he was gone.

But when he returned, he didn't speak.

He just helped me close the file.

We lifted the dusty, timeworn box and placed it back onto the shelf.

Putting it back was difficult.

But I had found him.

I had said goodbye.

As we stepped out of the records room and the door clicked shut behind us, I felt the weight of finality settle into my chest.

Jonathan was never lost.

He had just been waiting for me to find him.

And I had finally come.

Chapter 40
The Night I Saw Him

The Walk Back to My Room

Walking back to my room, my legs felt heavy, each step weighted by what I had just learned.

My body ached—not just from exhaustion, but from the weight pressing against my chest.

I could only take in a little at a time.

One thought repeated in my mind, steady and certain:

I found him.

As I stepped through the locked doors of 3L, I heard them click shut behind me.

The hallway was dark now, the usual hum of activity replaced by a heavy stillness.

The air smelled faintly of antiseptic—and something else.

Something quieter.

Like the ghost of a lullaby.

For the first time, it didn't feel like a place I feared.

It was just... quiet.

I whispered the words aloud, as if speaking them into existence would help me believe:

"He was here. Nurses and doctors tried to save him."

Ahead of me, my therapist disappeared down the dim hallway, but I stood there for a moment longer, letting the truth settle inside me.

Someone else had cared.

Someone else had tried to help him.

I hadn't been there—but others had.

The thought was painful and oddly comforting all at once.

A strange kind of peace, knowing he hadn't been alone.

Facing the Window Again

I closed my door behind me and left the overhead light off.

In the darkness, I sat at the edge of my bed, letting it all sink in.

Tonight, the view outside would not be like any other night.

I changed into my nightgown, crossed the cold floor barefoot, and paused.

Tears welled in my eyes before I even reached the window.

Slowly, I pressed my fingertips against the glass, tracing the invisible barrier that had separated me from the truth for so long.

A whisper rose up inside me:

I missed you. I missed it all.

And I gazed down at the nursery.

Not Just Looking. Seeing.

For three days, Jonathan had been right there.

Right there, fighting for his life.

The place I had stared at for weeks—absently, distantly—had never meant anything to me.

Until now.

Now, I saw it.

The rows of baby bassinets.

The soft glow of overhead lights.

The quiet movements of nurses tending to newborns.

I pressed my forehead against the cold glass, my breath fogging up a small patch in front of me.

Tears spilled down, blending into the chill of the window.

I imagined him there.

His tiny body, wrapped in a blanket.

His soft, sweet head with just a little bit of hair.

The familiar powdery scent of him, the warmth of his fragile body curled against my chest.

The few precious moments I had held him.

Before today, the nursery had just been another part of the hospital—a place I looked at without really seeing.

But tonight was different.

Tonight, I didn't just look at the nursery.

I saw it.

I stood there for a long time, my forehead resting against the glass, my body aching with both grief and closeness.

Jonathan had been here.

And somehow, in the stillness of this night, he was here still.

A Whisper Into the Night

Outside, the sky stretched out, endless and quiet, the stars scattered like distant pinpricks of light.

I stared into the night, then down at the nursery, feeling a connection I had never thought possible.

I closed my eyes for a moment, letting the silence wrap around me.

Then, in the softest voice, I whispered:

"I love you, baby boy."
My chest tightened.
My arms ached with the memory of his weight.
And in that moment, standing at the window,
I wasn't just remembering.
I was holding him.

Chapter 41
Especially The
Broken Parts

S omewhere deep inside, a quiet strength stirred—ready to carry me forward into whatever came next.

Days passed in a gentle blur.

I stayed mostly to myself, letting the truth I had uncovered settle inside me.

I kept thinking about that dusty box in the hospital basement.

The sound of the lid creaking open.

The sight of his name on that fragile page.

I had gone there not knowing if I could face the truth.

But I found it.

I found him.

And somehow, even in the pain of it, something inside me had shifted—made room for peace.

Then, the day came.

The day they told me I was being released to go home.

I packed the small pieces of my life into the suitcase—some clothes, a notebook, a worn paperback tucked between the folds.

It didn't seem like much.

But I knew I was carrying far more than what fit in my hands.

I was carrying the beginnings of healing.

The pieces of love, grief, memory—and the fragile hope that somehow, step by step, I could find my way home again.

Before I left, I stood for a moment just inside my room, taking one last look around.

The blank white walls.

The sturdy twin bed.

The heavy window that had framed so many silent nights.

And the spot by the glass where I had finally seen the nursery—and finally seen him.

I hadn't realized it then, but going to the window had changed something deep inside me.

It hadn't erased the grief.

But it had softened the edges.

It had shown me that even when I couldn't be there, love had been there.

It still was.

And after everything—after the screams, the silence, the unraveling, and the moment my own body refused to continue—something in me was finally ready to try.

I closed my suitcase, lifted the handle, and stepped out into the hallway.

The long corridor stretched out before me, sterile and familiar.

I walked slowly, the wheels of my suitcase thudding softly against the linoleum with each step.

When I reached the exit doors of 3L, I paused, glancing back one last time.

There was no grand moment—just a quiet goodbye in my heart.

As I crossed the threshold, the doors swung shut behind me.

And with a final, decisive click, they locked.

There were four of us leaving 3L that day—each with our own stories, our own scars, and our own therapists standing nearby. My therapist came to the lobby to say goodbye. He looked me in the eye and said, "You've done an incredible amount of work here."

He told me I had faced things most people spend years avoiding.

And then, with quiet conviction, he added,

"I want you to keep moving forward. Stay in counseling for at least a year. You've started something important here—now it's time to keep building on it, and if possible, I'd like you to take ninety days to be alone. Taking time for yourself and focusing on everything we've started here is going to be a major piece in your healing process."

His words stayed with me.

Stepping Outside

The air hit my face with a softness I hadn't felt in weeks.

Cool.

Fresh.

Real.

I blinked up at the light, my eyes adjusting to the brightness of it all.

It felt like stepping into a different world.

Leah walked beside me, matching my pace, saying nothing. She didn't need to.

She had been there all along—in her own way—waiting until I was ready.

We reached the car, and I turned to glance back at the hospital.

Not to hold on.

But to honor what had happened there.

I wasn't walking away from myself.

I was walking forward with everything I had gathered.

Even the broken parts.

Especially the broken parts.

The Ride Home

The first hour passed mostly in silence.

The rhythm of the road, the hum of tires on pavement, the faint music playing from the radio—It gave us space.

Leah didn't fill the silence.

She just drove, steady and calm, as if she knew that silence was a kind of medicine too.

I stared out the window, watching the evergreen trees and endless stretch of road blur past, my thoughts as scattered as the winter light.

Eventually, she glanced over at me.

"You ready to be home?" she asked, her voice soft.

I took a breath.

"Sort of."

The truth sat heavy in my chest, but I found the words.

"The hospital asked me to live alone for three months. To stay in therapy for at least a year."

Leah nodded slowly, keeping her eyes on the road.

"They said I need time. Time to recenter. To really work through everything I uncovered there."

She didn't speak right away.

She just reached over and gave my hand a gentle squeeze.

"You're doing the right thing," she said quietly.

I looked back out the window, following the lines of the landscape, the soft outlines of hills fading into the distance.

"I'm going to tell the girls when I get home," I said. "Let them know they'll be staying with their dad for now. We'll still see each other... but I need this time."

Leah nodded again, no judgment in her voice. Only understanding.

"You need this time to start healing. You are a good mom, never forget that," she said.

And for the first time in a long time, I believed her.

We drove on, the road unwinding before us, carrying me closer to a life I was just beginning to rebuild.

Closer to a home that wasn't just a place—but a new beginning.

Chapter 42
A Space to Heal

The apartment felt smaller than I remembered.

Maybe it hadn't changed.

Maybe I had.

I stood just inside the front door, suitcase still in hand, the silence settling around me like a heavy blanket.

The air smelled faintly of old carpet and forgotten corners.

It was cold. I crossed the room and turned up the thermostat on the wall.

Before even taking off my jacket, I dropped onto the couch and looked around.

I had been in an entirely different world.

Now the place I called home felt foreign—like I had stumbled into a life that no longer fit.

Everything that had happened on 3L felt surreal.

As if it had taken place on another planet.

Or inside someone else's skin.

Where do I go from here?

What will my first steps look like, now that I'm out in the world without the structure and safety of the hospital?

My thoughts vanished as I remembered the call I still needed to make—to my girls.

The apartment finally warmed enough for me to slip off my jacket.

I was excited.

Anxious.

Unsure of how they'd react to the three-month plan.

To my right stood the dining room, where the old oak table waited—the one I had sanded down years ago with the girls' father.

Its surface still held the marks of time, the soft wear of family meals and late-night conversations.

We had restored it together during a different season of life, when everything felt uncertain—but we were still trying.

Now it stood steady.

A quiet witness to everything that had come since.

One Deep Breath

I walked into the kitchen and turned on the kettle—not for tea, but for the comfort of a normal sound.

The click. The hum. The slow build of steam.

Something familiar to anchor me.

The hospital had asked me to live alone for three months.

To stay in therapy for at least a year.

To keep working through the memories I had unearthed—the grief I had finally allowed myself to feel.

They were giving me space to stay in the process.

Now, I had to give that space to myself.

But first—I had to call the girls.

Dialing the Number

I sat on the edge of my bed with the phone in my lap, staring at the digits for a long moment before pressing them in.

I had already talked this through with Leah.

And with my therapist.

Still, my hands trembled slightly as the line rang.

Rose answered first.

"Hi, honey," I said softly.

"Mama!" Her voice lit up through the receiver. "Are you home?"

"I am," I replied. "I just walked in. It's good to be back."

There was a pause. "Are we coming to see you?"

I swallowed hard.

"We're going to see each other every weekend," I said gently. "But not today."

Another pause.

"The hospital asked me to live alone for a little while—to stay focused on healing and continue therapy. They want me to keep working on everything I started while I was there."

"But we can come home later?" she asked.

"Yes, baby. You'll be home. Just not right away."

A Hard but Loving Choice

I talked to each of them—Mary, Ann, and Rose.

I explained in the simplest words I could.

That I was okay.

That I missed them terribly.

That they'd be staying with their dad for the next three months.

And that we'd see each other on weekends.

And that I loved them.

So much.

Each conversation was different, but the ache was the same.

It wasn't just a goodbye.

It was a boundary.

A hard one.

But a loving one.

I was doing this for them, too.

Because they deserved the version of me who had truly begun to heal.

Quiet Again

After the last call, I sat in the silence, the phone still in my lap.

A breeze moved through the cracked window, lifting the edge of the curtain.

Outside, the light was changing—late afternoon melting into dusk.

I wrapped my arms around myself and let the quiet settle again.

I didn't know what the coming weeks would look like.

I only knew I would keep showing up—one call,

one weekend,

one moment at a time.

I was where I needed to be.

And for now, that was enough.

Chapter 43
It's Ok Mom

The pizza was on fire.

Not just burnt—flaming.

Smoke filled the kitchen and rolled into the living room like fog, and for a moment, it felt like the whole apartment was coming undone.

But that wasn't how the visit started.

It started with a knock at the door.

My heart thundered in my chest as I opened it.

And there they they were—my girls.

Rose was the first to run in, arms wide, voice bright.

"Mommy! Mommy! Mommy, I'm so glad—Mommy!" she cried, throwing herself into my arms with all the joy and urgency of a seven-year-old who had waited too long.

I held her close, burying my face in her shoulder, blinking back tears.

Then came Ann.

She didn't say a word.

She just wrapped her arms around me in a long, quiet hug.

I kissed the top of her head and whispered, "How's my little Brown Bear doing?"

She nodded gently, her face still pressed against me.

Yes, she was doing good.

Marie was last.

Her hug wasn't as tight.

A little more cautious.

A little more distant.

But I understood.

Marie had been through the most with me.

She had heard the late-night fights through closed doors.

She had lived through the divorce in a way her younger sisters didn't.

She carried things I hadn't been ready to face—until now.

A Visit Full of Hope (and Smoke)

I was nervous and excited to see them all.

I wanted the visit to go perfectly.

I had picked up their favorite pizza, paper cups, and even root beer.

After about an hour of settling in—catching up, laughing, and letting them explore the space—I put the pizza in the oven.

And then I remembered.

I had smoked a cigarette upstairs earlier that day—one of the few moments I had given in since coming home.

I wasn't proud of it.

I had quit smoking seven years earlier, proud to leave it behind.

But somewhere in the haze of grief and confusion at the hospital—on one of the hardest days, when the weight of everything felt like too much—I found myself sitting in the designated smoking area on 3L, bumming cigarettes off the others like an old habit I thought I had buried.

It wasn't who I wanted to be.

But healing wasn't a straight line.

And sometimes, even survival came with its own tangled victories and setbacks.

While the pizza cooked, I crept upstairs to open the window wider and air it out, hoping they wouldn't notice.

I stood there, guilty and flustered, when something tugged at my gut.

The pizza.

I raced down the stairs—but it was too late.

Smoke filled the kitchen.

I had forgotten to take the cardboard off the bottom, and it had caught fire inside the oven.

Thick, gray smoke billowed out as the edges of the pizza blackened and curled.

Ann flew into action—racing to the back door, throwing it open, and fanning it with her arms.

Marie grabbed a towel, holding it out like maybe she could help.

Rose tapped me gently on the arm and said, *"It's okay, Mom."*

I grabbed the potholders, yanked the flaming pizza from the oven, and slid it onto the stovetop, blowing on the edges like it would help.

I stood there, winded.

Embarrassed.

Trying not to cry.

And yet—there they were.

Ann, still flapping the back door like a determined little firefighter.

Marie, standing steady, watching me without anger.

And Rose... sweet Rose... smiling up at me with a quiet kind of grace.

"It's okay, Mom."

It wasn't the night I had planned.

But it was real.

One Moment at a Time

We opened windows.

We laughed a little.

I scraped the worst of the crust off and promised them cereal and root beer for dinner instead.

Later, we painted nails.

Ann picked pink.

Rose wanted glitter.

Marie didn't say much—but she let me braid her hair.

That night, after they were asleep, I sat in the quiet.

I didn't have all the answers.

I wasn't fully healed.

I had just nearly lit dinner on fire.

But I was here.

And I was finding my way back to them.

One hug.

One mistake.

One moment at a time.

Chapter 44
She Kept Reaching

They were my reason for getting up.

For choosing help.

For finding the strength to heal.

Even after the girls left that night, the smell of burnt pizza lingering in the air and root beer cans clinking in the trash, I sat in the quiet, thinking about them—about all the reasons I had fought to come home.

I pulled a blanket around my shoulders, leaned back against the couch, and let their faces fill my mind—each so different, each so precious.

Their voices were still alive in the room, stitched into the silence.

This healing was for them.

For Marie

My first call had been with Marie.

She had been my first in so many ways.

She wasn't my first child—Jonathan was.

My beautiful boy who never got to grow up.

Who left this world far too soon in that horrific car accident.

But Marie was the first I got to raise.

The first to call me "Mom" in the ordinary, everyday ways that break your heart and bloom it all at once.

The first scraped knees.

The first bedtime stories.

The first tiny victories that made the world tilt back into focus.

She was fitted with her first prosthetic hook at just nine months old—and from the beginning, she had a will of steel.

She adapted before she could even speak—learning to tie shoes one-handed, hold crayons, open doors, navigate the stares and whispers of kids who didn't understand.

She never asked to be strong.

But she was.

She didn't complain.

She didn't want sympathy.

She just wanted to live like any other little girl.

And she did.

More than live—she thrived.

I'll never forget the first time she caught the school bus on her own.

She wore her little red coat and matching goulashes, her backpack bouncing behind her as she walked down the sidewalk.

I stood at the window and watched her climb the steps, head held high, never looking back.

My heart swelled and ached all at once.

One of those forever moments a mother tucks away in her bones.

She was ready—even if I wasn't.

Later, she joined baton twirling—and quickly became a standout.

At just eight years old, she stole the show.

She performed at the local high school with the other girls, twirling with confidence as the music filled the auditorium.

I sat in the audience—a proud mama—watching as the spotlight found her and stayed.

The crowd didn't see the hook.

They saw her grace.

Her confidence.

Her joy.

And so did I.

I held my breath as she moved across the floor, her baton arcing through the air and landing cleanly back in her hand.

She never looked nervous. She never hesitated.

She shined.

She was proud of herself.

And I was proud of her.

One of the reasons she always stood out was the outfits.

They weren't store-bought. They were magic.

My high school friend Paula was an exceptional seamstress. She loved sewing holiday dresses for the girls—bright greens for Christmas, pinks and hearts for Valentine's Day—but baton costumes? Those were her favorite.

She poured her creativity into every stitch, designing custom twirling outfits that shimmered under stage lights and turned heads in every crowd.

Paula made sure Marie's baton outfits were the best.

And when Marie stepped out—confident, radiant, spinning her baton with that familiar glint in her eye—you could feel the pride ripple through the room.

A New Possibility

Then came the turning point.

I was working part-time when I met an older couple who began stopping by my workplace every so often. They were kind, engaging—easy to talk to. Each time they visited, we'd chat a little longer.

Around the same time, Marie—fifteen years old then—had seen something on TV about a new kind of prosthetic hand offered through Shriners Hospital for Children. She was intrigued.

Hopeful. It planted a seed.

And then one afternoon, during one of those friendly conversations at work, the couple mentioned they were Shriners.

I blinked.

It felt like one of those rare, perfect synchronicities—the kind you can't make up.

I told them about Marie. About the TV segment. About how she had quietly begun wondering if that kind of prosthetic could be possible for her too.

They didn't hesitate.

They offered to write a letter on Marie's behalf and introduce her to the Chief of Staff at the Shriners hospital located three hours away.

What started as a conversation in an ordinary office turned into the extraordinary beginning of something we had barely dared to hope for.

The Drives and the Decision

We found ourselves driving together over the mountain pass—just the two of us.

Those drives became sacred: winding roads filled with quiet conversations, nervous laughter, and a deepening bond that only comes from shared strength.

At Shriners, she met with the Chief of Staff. A short visit, with another appointment set for one month later.

Then came the big day—the decision.

She stood beside me, calm and composed.

We had already been through the medical evaluation. Now we were here for something different—this was the vote. The decision-making process.

The room looked more like a small stadium than a clinic, with tiered seating rising around us. I sat beside Marie at the front, and for a moment, I looked up—twelve doctors seated in rows, their faces calm, clinical, focused.

The Chief of Staff stood at a podium, speaking into a microphone that crackled softly. His voice carried through the room with gentle authority as he looked over the assembled panel.

Then he paused.

And with the smallest smile, he asked:

"How many of you think it's time this beautiful redheaded sixteen-year-old had a hand?"

Every hand shot up—quickly, decisively.

Right there. A unanimous yes.

Tears blurred my vision.

Marie and I stood up.

I stepped forward to thank them, my voice cracking—but I didn't care.

Gratitude filled every inch of me.

After everything we had been through—here we were.

Here she was.

The Chief turned to me gently.

"Mom, why don't you wait in the hall while we talk more with Marie?"

He knew I needed the space to feel the fullness of it all—and she needed the moment to be hers.

I gave her a soft nod and stepped out.

I leaned against the hallway wall, chest full, letting the tears fall freely.

That day, they didn't just give her a hand.

They gave her dignity.

Recognition.

A future that felt wide open.

When she walked out, there was a quiet joy on her face.

The kind that said something inside her had shifted.

Becoming

Shriners became a beginning.

Marie would no longer wear a hook.

She would have a hand—and with it, a new kind of confidence.

She kept rising.

After everything—the Shriners visits, the fittings, the uncertainty—Marie stepped forward into her life with purpose.

She didn't let her story stop at survival.

She kept reaching.

She went on to complete her college degree—a milestone that felt like a full-circle moment for both of us.

I thought back to the little girl in red goulashes, beaming with fierce independence.

She grew into a capable, compassionate, determined woman—The kind who walks into a room and truly sees people.

She had been my fire—And my fiercest teacher.

Through her, I learned one of life's deepest truths:

Healing isn't about erasing the past.

It's about becoming strong enough to carry it—with grace.

Chapter 45
Relax Mom.
I've Got It

After I had my call with Marie, I had talked with Ann. My Brown Bear.

Bold. Bright. Fearless in ways only a middle child can be.

She was six—just a little girl with a big personality and even bigger questions.

When she picked up the phone, her voice was light and bright.

"Hi Mommy!"

That alone made me tear up.

There wasn't the same hesitation I'd heard in Marie's voice.

Ann was too young to carry that kind of fear yet.

But there was still something in her tone that made my heart ache.

Like she knew I'd been gone longer than usual.

Like she missed me, but didn't quite know how to say it.

"I miss you, Brown Bear," I whispered, using the nickname I always called her.

Her brunette hair and darker complexion had set her apart from Marie's and Rose's redheads—but it was more than that.

She had a bold spirit.

A fire all her own.

"I miss you too, Mommy," she said. "Can we have pancakes when I come home?"

I could practically see her big brown eyes smiling through the phone.

Ann was my middle daughter—the one always climbing, jumping, tumbling, and falling.

If she wasn't on top of something, she was halfway off it.

Fearless.

Curious.

Constantly in motion.

She once fell off a playhouse and broke her leg—wore the cast like it was part of her superhero costume.

She stuffed peas up her nose just to see what would happen.

I had to sit her down and have her blow and blow until they shot across the room.

She thought it was hilarious.

She loved playing dress-up—feather boas, plastic heels, tulle skirts trailing behind her like royalty.

And later, I found out she and Marie had unwrapped all their Christmas gifts early one year, then carefully rewrapped them.

Marie may have been the ringleader, but Ann was definitely in on it.

At three years old, we were walking down the sidewalk at the Oregon Coast.

She wore a tiny two-piece bathing suit, marching ahead of me like she owned the town.

Then she turned, swinging her hips, flashed a mischievous smile, and said, "You're despicable!" —giggling all the way, without the slightest clue what the word meant.

As a teenager, she was just as bold.

One time, she asked if she could go to McDonald's with her cousin.

I said yes, assuming she meant the one ten minutes away.

She meant the one two hours away.

She didn't even flinch when I found out. Just looked at me like, Well... you didn't ask which McDonald's.

Then there was the time I told her she couldn't stay out past curfew.

She came home around 10 p.m. that night—cool, casual, all smiles. Said goodnight, dropped her bag, and headed to her room like she had nothing to hide.

And for a minute, I bought it.

But something about the way she was too cooperative made me suspicious. So around 10:30, I peeked into her room.

The bed was empty.

She'd gone out the window.

So I did what any tired, slightly over-it mom would do:

I crawled into her bed and waited.

She had a friend staying over that night—Leah. Sweet, fun, charming... and just as sneaky as Ann. I had said yes to the sleepover because they claimed they were "studying."

Yeah, right.

Around 1 a.m., the two of them came climbing back in through the window like a pair of awkward ninjas.

And there I was—already in the bed, arms crossed, waiting like the surprise ending they never saw coming.

They froze.

No one moved. No one spoke.

I didn't yell. I didn't lecture. I just said—calm and steady:

"If you're going to sneak out after curfew, don't come back just to pretend you were here. Maybe next time... just stay out."

That was all.

They knew they were busted.

And even though I was furious, a small part of me wasn't the least bit surprised.

Leah was the perfect accomplice—equal parts clever and fearless. They made a great team... just not that night.

It was classic Ann—sneaky, determined, always pushing limits.

But she wasn't just bold—she was capable.

When I couldn't set up the camping tent, she'd mutter, "Oh Mom," and come do it herself.

If her car broke down in high school, she'd pop the hood and figure it out.

She didn't panic.

She didn't whine.

She just handled it.

Even as a little girl, I could see that spark in her—the way she moved through the world without hesitation.

The way she ran toward things other kids would tiptoe around.

She and Rose were only eighteen months apart and shared the same bedroom.

When Rose was brand new, still in a bassinet, I'd go in during the night when she cried—and there would be Ann, wide-eyed and grinning from her crib, bouncing up and down with her arms stretched toward me.

I started to wonder if Ann was waking her sister up on purpose—just so she could be scooped up and brought into bed with me too.

And honestly?

I wouldn't put it past her.

Even then, she knew how to work the system—with charm and timing that were nothing short of impressive.

Out of all my girls, Ann looks the most like me.

Same smile.

Same spark in the eyes when she's up to something.

People would say, 'She's your twin,' and I'd laugh—especially when she pulled one of her sneaky tricks and I caught myself thinking, Me? Sneaky?

Maybe she got it from me.

Maybe I just recognized myself in her boldness.

In our little trio of daughters, she was the bridge.

The middle one.

She could rile up her sisters in one breath—and defend them in the next.

Marie would roll her eyes; Rose would follow her lead—and Ann somehow balanced chaos and care all at once.

As an adult, Ann is exactly who she always was becoming.

Disciplined.

Hardworking.

Fiercely loyal.

Practical to the bone, but with a heart as wide as the sky.

She'll roll her eyes at you—then show up at your door with a toolbox and a solution.

She is still my Brown Bear—strong, steady, and wild in all the right ways.

She keeps me on my toes—even now.

But she also keeps me grounded.

My Brown Bear.

My mirror.

My reminder that strength doesn't always roar—

Sometimes, it climbs through windows with a smile and says,

"Relax, Mom. I've got this."

Chapter 46
Five Pings and a Heart

My last call had been with Rose.

If Ann was my fearless climber, Rose was my storm.

Fierce.

Beautiful.

Unpredictable.

And sometimes—heartbreakingly hard to reach.

After I spoke to Ann, I asked to speak to Rose.

My youngest—so full of personality.

So much drive to live life, even at six years old.

"Hi Mommy. When can we come home? I miss you."

"I know, baby girl. I miss you too."

Rose was the one who'd be in mud puddles after school.

I remember pulling up to the elementary school one afternoon just as the snowmelt had pooled into deep potholes.

Out of the corner of my eye, I saw a little girl—dress hiked up, splashing in a giant puddle.

No boots.

Just anklets and soaked school shoes.

I remember thinking, Oh, the poor mom of that one.

Then I looked again—and realized I was that poor mom.

Rose's muddy little body climbed into the car, dripping and grinning.

Ann slid in beside her, laughing.

"Mom, Rose is sure muddy."

"Yes," I sighed. "So I noticed."

That was Rose.

Testing life.

Diving into it—dress and all.

She had always been a firecracker.

Vivacious.

Redheaded.

Full of spirit.

Athletic, popular, fearless.

She made people laugh.

Lit up any room.

Charged down soccer fields without hesitation.

She was smart, funny, magnetic.

There was a light in her that everyone noticed.

But sometime around middle school, the light began to flicker.

At first, it was subtle—less laughter, more walls.

Mood swings sharper than the usual teenage storms.

Then came high school.

And everything shifted.

Drugs.

First marijuana.

Then stronger.

She started having outbursts in class—emotional, sometimes aggressive, unpredictable moments that left teachers and classmates stunned.

People talked.

They knew something was wrong, even if they didn't know exactly what.

And when she was pulled from school and sent away, everyone noticed.

Everyone knew—or thought they knew.

She was placed in a school that operated more like a lockdown facility, three hours from home.

By that time, her sisters had already graduated.

I moved to the valley to be closer—away from the mountain passes, the long drives—so I could show up when she needed me most.

The school wasn't just a place to finish high school.

It was a place to stabilize.

To detox.

To remove the drugs and alcohol from her system.

To find the right medication so her mind could begin to settle and focus again.

It wasn't easy.

But it was necessary.

And through it all—she kept going.

She wanted to walk with her class.

And she did.

She walked back into the same school where everyone had seen her fall apart.

Into the same hallways where people whispered and judged and wondered what happened to her.

She walked across that stage—cap and gown, tassel swaying, chin high.

I watched from the audience, so proud I could barely breathe.

After Rose graduated from high school, she came to live with me in the city. At nineteen, she seemed solid—she was taking her medication, working full-time, and had quickly become the top salesperson in her department at one of the city's largest retail stores. We were even attending counseling sessions together.

Having a third-party professional involved was something I felt strongly about—it was one of the boundaries I set. If she was going to live with me, we needed someone outside our dynamic to help us both.

In one of those early sessions, the psychologist—a soft-spoken, middle-aged woman—did something I'll never forget. She handed each of us a shoebox. Between us sat a stack of folded pieces of paper, each one labeled with a different responsibility.

She turned to Rose and said, "I'm going to read each responsibility out loud. If it belongs to you, it goes in your box. If it's your mother's, it goes in hers."

We began.

As the stack dwindled, my box remained mostly empty.

At the end of the session, I looked down and saw just two slips of paper in front of me:

Provide a roof over her head.

Make sure there is food to eat.

Everything else—taking medication, respecting her mother, doing her laundry, being on time, staying sober, staying off drugs, keeping her bathroom clean—belonged to Rose.

It was simple. And transformative.

That session was the beginning of my letting go—not of love, but of ownership over her life. I didn't have to carry it all. I wasn't responsible for her every action, choice, or failure. And seeing that laid out so clearly changed something in me.

It helped me step back with clarity and compassion.

At work Rose was magnetic with customers—quick-witted, confident, and charming.

Everyone at her job loved her.

She was being responsible for her own life.

And I was so proud.

But then...

Drugs were offered.

And she said yes.

It started slowly.

Almost invisibly.

But before long, the spiral began again—steeper this time.

That's when we began placing her in group homes all over the state.

Every time, we hoped it would stick.

And every time, she was asked to leave.

The illness, the rage, the addiction—it was too much for them.

Eventually, there were no more options nearby.

We had to transfer her to a group home in a neighboring state.

That's where she was when I started organizing the Christmas parties.

When Everything Shattered

And then, one day, everything shattered.

During a spiral none of us saw coming, Rose attempted to take her own life.

She cut her throat from ear to ear.

Her wrists too.

The phone call still echoes inside me.

She survived.

By some miracle—she survived.

After surgery and a long, difficult recovery, she was transferred to the state hospital.

That was the moment everything changed.

Not quickly.

Not cleanly.

But it was a turning point.

A line in the sand between the chaos and the long road to stability that would follow.

Eventually, Rose was diagnosed with schizoaffective disorder—A condition that includes symptoms of schizophrenia and mood disorders.

Her manic episodes made her feel invincible one moment and furious the next.

Her rage wasn't who she was—It was how the illness showed up before we had the words for it.

Before we had the tools to understand.

That's the part no one talks about.

The part that kept us apart.

The Years That Followed

There were nights we got phone calls at 2 a.m.—from group homes, hospitals, parking lots in the middle of nowhere.

And without hesitation, we were out the door.

Every time.

No matter what horror waited on the other side.

My new husband never flinched.

He hadn't raised her. He hadn't lived through the years of chaos.

But he never asked why.

He just grabbed his coat and stood beside me.

This wasn't his daughter by blood.

But you wouldn't have known it.

He carried her crisis like it was ours.

Because it was.

In the middle of all that heartbreak, I found NAMI—the National Alliance on Mental Illness. Doug and I had only been married two years when I joined their Family-to-Family classes. And something remarkable happened—he came with me. Week after week, we sat side by side, learning how to love someone through the storms of mental illness. What began as a class quickly became a lifeline, giving us tools, language, and hope we didn't know we were missing.

How to help without losing ourselves.

How to breathe when the bottom dropped out.

At our first meeting, one of the leaders looked at Doug and said:

"You're taking on someone else's daughter—someone who's struggling with mental illness. That's a rare kind of courage."

The room applauded.

He didn't flinch.

He just smiled and said,

"I support her in whatever she needs."

And he meant it.

Later, I began teaching the NAMI class.

I stood in rooms full of wide-eyed parents, numb siblings, heartbroken spouses.

And I recognized them all.

I knew their pain.

And I finally had something to offer:

A way forward.

The Christmas Parties

I organized a Christmas party every year for families affected by mental illness—those who otherwise had no holiday, no place to go.

I raised the money myself.

Reached out to local businesses for donations.

Gathered gifts for every adult and child.

There were tables piled with presents.

A full turkey dinner.

Santa Claus.

Live entertainment.

My dearest friends volunteered each year to help.

And every December, the line outside grew longer—families standing in the cold for hours, waiting for a warm seat, a hot meal, and a place to feel seen.

It became one of the most meaningful things I had ever done.

Eventually, the City of Vancouver awarded me a plaque.

It read: The Power of One.

Rose never got to attend those Christmas parties herself.

She lived too far away.

But every gift, every meal, every moment of belonging—I held her in my heart.

Because even when I couldn't fix everything for her,

I could still create a little light in the darkness.

For others.

For myself.

For her.

And Then... Hope

We drove to visit Rose often when she was placed out of state—five hours away.

Sometimes she could talk.

Sometimes she couldn't.

But we came anyway.

She never attended those Christmas parties.

But in a way—they were for her, too.

For the version of her lost behind fear and illness.

For others like her who had no one.

For years, I couldn't give Rose peace.
So I gave it to others like her.
And then...
Slowly...
Things began to change.
Not quickly.
Not magically.
But steadily.
In the last ten years, something in Rose has settled.
The right medication.
The right support.
Maybe just... the right time.
She got married.
She built a more stable life.
She still lives with schizo-affective disorder
But she lives with it now.
Not under it.
She is doing phenomenal.
Not perfect.
Not cured.
But standing.
Alive.
Present.
Herself.

Five Pings

She sends me text messages almost every day.
Always the same:
A soft ping.
Then another.

And another.

And another.

Four photos—usually of something simple. Something she saw and wanted to share:

A flower. A landscape. A cloud. A quirky sign. Her cat curled up in a funny position.

And then, the fifth ping:

"I love you."

And a heart.

And after everything?

That's everything.

Chapter 47
One Hour at a Time

I had spent so long trying to be strong for my daughters.

But now, with the girls staying with their dad and the apartment echoing with silence, it was time to figure out who I was when I wasn't holding anyone else up.

That meant sitting in the quiet.

That meant showing up.

One hour at a time.

The car coughed as I turned the key.

My silver Chevy Citation—lovingly nicknamed The Gutless Wonder—shuddered before settling into a low, wheezing idle.

My brother-in-law, George, had found it for me in the city.

It wasn't glamorous—in fact, I felt like I was driving a silver egg down the road—but I appreciated what he had done for me.

It was paid for.

And it was mine.

I had just bought it with the small inheritance my mother left behind—money I hadn't been able to touch until I turned thirty-five.

It wasn't much. Just enough for a used car and gas money.

The rest of the inheritance was already gone—used to pay off the creditors my ex-husband had listed in bankruptcy.

Most of them were family friends. People who had once known and respected my father.

The owner of the lumber yard where I grew up was one of them.

Even my seventy-five-year-old uncle—the one who had loaned us $8,000 years earlier—was legally included in the claim because he held a signed promissory note.

I didn't want their memory of my father—or their trust in our family—tied to unpaid debts.

So I drove to each place myself.

Looked them in the eye.

And paid them back.

It was a different kind of healing.

A different kind of strength.

The County Office

The building wasn't much to look at—beige metal siding, a peeling sign in the window.

Inside, fluorescent lights buzzed overhead. The air smelled faintly of dust and old carpet.

This was what the county offered: no frills, no candles, no essential oils—just two chairs, a chipped desk, and a woman with a clipboard who looked tired in the way only social workers do—like she had carried too many stories, but still had room for mine.

"Have a seat," she said gently.

I sat down and pulled my jacket tighter around me.

She asked the basics—intake questions, consent forms, boxes to check.

Then she looked up and asked, "What brings you in?"

"The hospital," I said. "They told me I needed to stay in therapy. For a year. They told me I needed to keep going."

She nodded. "And do you want to keep going?"

I hesitated.

"I do," I said finally. "But it's harder now.

Without the structure.

Without the nurses and locked doors and daily check-ins.

Now it's just me.

And the quiet."

That last word hung between us.

She didn't rush to fill it.

She let it settle.

What I Was Carrying

I talked about the girls.

The phone calls.

The decision to have them stay with their dad for three months while I continued healing.

The hospital's recommendation.

The way my apartment felt quieter than I expected.

I told her I had a Section 8 apartment. That I was grateful to have it.

That I was still unpacking more than just the suitcase I brought home—I was unpacking years.

She listened.

Really listened.

"You've been through a lot," she said softly.

"I have," I replied. "But I'm still here."

That year in therapy after the hospital was when I really started taking my power back.

My counselor helped me see that I didn't owe my ex-husband anything more.

Not conversation. Not guilt. Not another piece of my energy.

She gave me permission I didn't know I needed: that it was okay to stop feeding emotion into something that no longer served me.

She helped me visualize it in the most unexpected way.

Every time Dean would speak to me—whether on the phone or in person—I imagined myself inside a glass cubicle.

I could see him.

But his words hit the glass wall and bounced right off. They didn't reach me.

It might sound hokey, but it worked.

It gave me back control.

I stopped answering his calls.

I stopped explaining myself to someone who never truly listened.

His choices were his. Mine were mine.

And I finally understood: our decisions—our decisions alone—shape the course of our lives.

The Shift

One afternoon early in our sessions, I was talking—venting, really—about how unfair everything felt.

I was tired of being the one who always had to start over.

Tired of shouldering the consequences of other people's choices.

I had been spiraling through all the familiar frustrations: how much I had lost, how hard it was to rebuild, how exhausted I was from doing it all alone.

And that's when my counselor paused and asked,

"And what does that buy you?"

I blinked. My cheeks flushed.

I felt myself get defensive—angry, even.

Her words felt abrupt. Almost cold.

Did she not hear everything I had just said?

But I couldn't stop thinking about that question.

For days, it echoed in my mind.

She wasn't diminishing what I'd been through.

She was gently inviting me to look at how I was using my pain.

Without realizing it, I had been throwing myself a quiet little pity party.

Replaying the same injustices.

Clinging to the same stories—not because they healed me, but because they justified where I was stuck.

That realization—however painful—shifted something in me.

It helped me see not just what I was feeling, but how I was operating.

It forced me to ask hard questions:

Why am I telling this story this way?

What's keeping me tethered to this pain?

What am I avoiding by staying angry, or small, or right?

It was one of the first times I truly began to examine my own patterns and ask:

Is this helping me heal, or just helping me cope?

That subtle shift—just the beginning of that kind of self-honesty—was essential.

Healing, I began to understand, wasn't just about what had been done to me.

It was also about how I chose to move forward from it.

The Groups

Before I left one session, she handed me a short list of local support groups.

Some were for grief.

Some were for abuse.

All of them unfamiliar—and a little intimidating.

But I went.

I sat in cold metal chairs beside strangers.

Listened to stories that mirrored mine.

Spoke when I could.

Cried when I couldn't.

I felt like a ball of yarn unraveling—loose ends everywhere, tangled and exposed.

But I stayed with it.

Even when it was uncomfortable.

Even when I didn't feel ready.

And slowly,

I got better.

One Hour at a Time

At the end of my first session, the counselor asked,

"Would you like to come back next week?"

I nodded.

Because that's what healing looked like now.

Not perfect days or dramatic breakthroughs.

Not sweeping victories.

Just this.

One hour at a time.

One choice at a time.

One breath at a time.

And maybe, someday-

Peace.

Chapter 48
Already Loved

In those early days of healing, I went where I was guided—
Support groups, quiet rooms, community circles where grief and growth shared space.

One afternoon, I found myself sitting in a folding chair in a room that smelled like peppermint tea, surrounded by people who knew loss in their bones.

It was my second or third time attending the grief group. The chairs were arranged in a loose circle. The air was heavy with unspoken weight—guilt, regret, questions. The topic that day was forgiveness—not of others, but of ourselves.

One woman talked about blaming herself for her husband's death.

Another man said he hadn't made it in time to say goodbye to his brother.

Everyone had something they carried like a stone in their chest.

When it was my turn, I hesitated.

"I used to think I had done something wrong," I said slowly, my eyes fixed on a spot in the carpet.

"Like maybe all the hard things that happened to me were punishment. I mean... how else could I make sense of it all? It had to be because of something, right?"

The room grew quiet.

"I had been baptized in five different churches," I said folding my hands in my lap.

"All different denominations. Each one said, 'We're the way.' Each one promised peace if I followed their path. And I did. I followed. I obeyed. I submerged. I confessed. I showed up."

I paused.

"But it didn't work. Not for me. I kept waiting for something to lift, to change. And it never did."

A few people nodded, quietly.

"I kept thinking maybe it was me. Maybe I hadn't repented enough. Maybe I didn't believe hard enough. Maybe I was the problem."

I swallowed hard, remembering the hospital.

"While I was on 3L, I tried to go to the Catholic chapel on the lower floor. I stood outside the door three Sundays in a row. I couldn't go in. I'd just stand there, frozen. I don't even know what held me back—grief, shame, exhaustion, maybe all of it."

On my last day, a priest found me standing outside the chapel again.

He didn't quote scripture.

He didn't ask for confession.

He didn't ask anything.

He just put his arm gently around me and said, "All you need to know is... God is love."

That's it.

No theology.

No doctrine.

Just that.

God is love.

And in that moment, something happened I hadn't expected.

It felt like ten thousand pounds were lifted from my shoulders in an instant.

Not gradually. Not subtly.

It was immediate.

It was profound.

I hadn't expected it—hadn't even realized how heavy the weight had become until it vanished.

No theology had ever done that.

No sermon. No baptism. No checklist of spiritual "shoulds."

Just those three words.

Spoken gently.

Spoken with no expectation.

Spoken without a single demand to earn or prove or repent.

And in that quiet moment, something in me shifted permanently.

It didn't erase the pain.

But it changed how I carried it.

From that day forward, I began to understand:

Maybe healing didn't require perfection.

Maybe it just required love.

I hadn't failed.

I wasn't being punished.

I was just hurting.

And healing doesn't come from being dunked five times and trying harder to be holy.

It comes from knowing you are already loved.

A woman across the circle wiped her eyes. Someone else reached for my hand.

The truth had landed.

"I wish I could say the healing happened right then," I said softly. "But it didn't. Not all at once."

I paused.

"But it started there."

And sometimes, starting is enough.

Sometimes love doesn't come from a pulpit.

It comes from a hallway hug.

From a stranger's kindness.

From one simple truth whispered at the right moment.

God is love.

And for me, that was finally enough.

Chapter 49
Looking Back

Looking back on those days—when I was deep in counseling and local support groups—I see how much unseen work was happening beneath the surface. Healing wasn't a straight line. It wasn't tidy. There were no clear road signs pointing the way. Just long days, quiet moments, and an aching hope that the next right step would somehow reveal itself.

Two memories always surface at the same time when I think of that season: the intensity of the emotional labor I was doing, and the simple, quiet rituals I created to keep going.

I remember praying—not on my knees, not with folded hands, but in motion. I prayed while walking. My prayers weren't whispers—they were shouted words carried into the open air. I'd walk through a wide, empty field beside my apartment and let the words pour out of me.

Sometimes they were desperate. Sometimes angry. Sometimes pleading. I wasn't reciting anything polished. I was just speaking out loud—raw and unrehearsed—hoping the sky was listening.

There were no answers. No voices from above. But there was a strange comfort in saying it all out loud—naming the pain, the longing, the hope.

That field became a sacred space to me. I used to grip small rocks in my hand like questions I didn't know how to ask. I'd throw them—hard—as far as I could, trying to release the weight I was still carrying. I had taught myself to do that instead of swallowing the pain like I used to.

It was my way of not internalizing it anymore. Of letting it move through me and out.

Walking became my greatest tool. Step after step, I gave myself space to process all that had happened—especially the time in the hospital. Those walks gave me permission to feel.

Sometimes I cried. Sometimes I remembered things I didn't know I had buried. And sometimes I just breathed.

Now, years later, when I look back on that version of me, I wish I could wrap her in warmth and whisper, "Keep going. You're doing it." I wish I could lay a smoother path in front of her—but I know she had to walk the one she was on. Every rocky step helped shape the woman I eventually became.

And so I honor her—the girl in the field, the one who shouted prayers into the wind, who walked instead of knelt, who threw rocks instead of turning pain inward. She was learning how to live again, one hard-earned step at a time.

...She didn't have all the answers.

But she kept showing up.

And without even realizing it—she was getting ready.

Ready for the next step.

Ready for life again.

Chapter 50
Mexicali

C ounseling helped me find my voice again—slowly, cautiously, one
breath at a time.

Each support group meeting, each quiet conversation, chipped away
at the walls I had built around myself.

Little by little, I wasn't just surviving anymore.

I was learning to trust life again.

To trust myself.

And without even realizing it—the pieces weren't just coming together.

They were gaining momentum.

For the first time in a long time, I felt something more than hope.

I felt ready.

Ready to build.

Ready to try.

Ready to leap.

A new beginning wasn't just possible—it was already happening.

Finding the Next Step

I needed part-time work that would allow me to go to school three
days a week—and it had to be evening shifts on those same days.

Leah asked me a simple question:

"What are your favorite places to go in town?"

We met at a cozy coffee shop, our favorite spot, to enjoy a fresh cup of Joe and brainstorm my next step.

I laid a local newspaper on the smooth wooden table between us.

"I brought the most recent Help Wanted ads," I said, running my finger over the ink-smudged pages.

Leah took a slow sip of her coffee, then smiled.

"You need to find someplace fun—somewhere you actually like to go while going back to school."

I scanned the listings, feeling equal parts excitement and dread.

Retail? No.

Office work? Not now.

I needed something low-pressure.

Somewhere I wouldn't feel like a complete outsider after so much time away from the working world.

And then—

"Hey! Mexicali is hiring!"

Leah's head snapped up.

"Seriously?"

It was our favorite Mexican restaurant—the best place in town.

The food was incredible.

The margaritas legendary.

We knew several of the employees.

We had spent many evenings there, unwinding, laughing, and making memories.

Leah grabbed the newspaper from me.

"Where?"

"Right there," I said, pointing to the ad with an ink-stained finger.

Leah grinned.

"A hostess? That would be perfect for you! No pressure—just fun!"

I swallowed hard.

My voice came out in a whisper.

"I'm so nervous. Do you really think I can do it?"

Leah's smile softened.

"Of course you can.

You've come so far—this is just the next step."

She pointed to the ad again.

"It says the hours are flexible. It's a great place, and you'll be surrounded by people you already know. It's going to be okay."

I nodded, heart pounding.

That same night, I applied for the job.

The very next day, I was hired.

I would start in one week.

First Day Jitters

The owner himself met me at the front door on my first day.

The restaurant wasn't open yet, and he had unlocked the door just for me.

I shook his hand, hoping he couldn't sense my nervousness.

"One hour until opening," he said with a friendly nod.

"Let me show you the layout of the tables and how we like to seat people."

He was tall and handsome, with dark, thick hair, dressed professionally in slacks and a button-down shirt.

I had noticed him before on previous visits—moving between tables, greeting guests with ease.

Now, I was on the other side of it—not as a customer, but as part of the team.

I took a deep breath.

I was ready.

Or at least, I thought I was.

The Anxiety of My First Night

From the moment the doors opened, I felt completely overwhelmed.

Loud conversations.

Laughter.

The clatter of dishes and silverware.

The smell of sizzling fajitas filling the air.

I had barely learned the table map, and suddenly, I was seating guests, answering questions, smiling through the panic rising in my chest.

I could feel my heart pounding as I tried to stay composed, but by the end of the night, I was lightheaded and disoriented.

I made it home completely drained, my body still buzzing with nerves.

The next morning, I did something I hadn't done in a long time.

I called my doctor.

"I don't think I can do this," I admitted. "I felt so out of it. I got dizzy, and everything was moving too fast. What if I'm not ready?"

His response was simple.

"You fake it until you make it."

I blinked.

"That's it?"

"That's it," he said.

"It's going to feel uncomfortable at first. It's going to feel impossible some days.

But you keep showing up, and one day, it won't feel fake anymore.

One day, it'll just be your life."

The Turning Point

That conversation stuck with me as I walked into my next shift.

I wasn't suddenly confident.

The anxiety didn't disappear overnight.

But I kept showing up.

And little by little, I realized—

He was right.

I wasn't faking it.

I was doing it.

A Change of Aprons

That summer, after a full year of balancing college and hostessing, I knew I needed more income—and I was ready for more responsibility.

So I stepped into it.

I began bussing tables during the day, still hostessing at night. And just a few days in, while hurrying past the owner's table, he stopped me mid-step.

"I need a daytime manager." he said. "Want the job?"

I said yes without hesitation.

"Good," he smiled. "Go take the apron off. You're done bussing tables."

It was that simple.

And that profound.

A few weeks later, he caught me thumbing through a sticky cocktail recipe book behind the bar—squinting, flipping pages, trying to figure out how to mix something halfway decent for a lunch guest. I must've looked completely lost.

He didn't say much—just raised an eyebrow that told me everything.

"You're going to bartending school," he said. "I'm paying."

I looked at him, silently laughing at myself.

I knew I was in over my head.

I also knew I'd figure it out.

So I did.

A Little Laughter Along the Way

The instructor at bartending school happened to be the husband of my coworker and good friend Teresa, which made the whole experience feel a little less intimidating—and a lot more hilarious.

It didn't take long for the jokes to start.

During our final exam—an otherwise silent, serious room filled with students bent over their papers—I accidentally let out a loud fart.

Without missing a beat, I pointed to the poor guy sitting next to me and said,

"He did it!"

The entire room erupted into laughter.

I laughed too—really laughed—not out of nervousness or fear of judgment, but because it was genuinely funny.

It felt good to laugh.

To not take myself so seriously.

To feel like part of the human race again.

At our next class, as the instructor handed out the graded exams, he couldn't resist teasing me one more time.

He walked over with a grin, slapped my test down on the desk with a big red A+ on top, and said loudly for everyone to hear:

"Lennie got an A+... but that's only because she slept with the instructor!"

The room howled with laughter again.

I shook my head, blushing and laughing right along with them.

There was no shame in it.

Just friendship.

Joy.

Normalcy.

And for the first time in a long time,

I realized healing didn't just happen in therapy sessions and quiet walks.

Sometimes, healing looked like laughing until you cried in a classroom full of strangers.

Sometimes, healing looked like being part of the joke—and loving every second of it.

Sometimes, healing looked like claiming your own voice, even in the middle of something messy and loud and human.

Chapter 51
Not Just Surviving

B efore the bartending classes, before managing day shifts at Mexicali, and before I truly began to feel steady on my feet—there was that first year.

It was the year I returned to school—starting at the community college to finally earn my high school diploma.

It began at the same time I started hostessing when everything still felt uncertain and new. I was juggling school, work, and motherhood, barely making ends meet—but I was also learning how to live again.

That first year didn't come with any grand transformation.

It came in small pieces.

And piece by piece, something began to change.

The pieces of my life were starting to fit together in ways I never imagined.

By day, I was a college student. By night, a restaurant hostess. And on weekends, I cleaned vacation rentals and motels to help make ends meet. Sometimes, I brought my youngest daughters with me—setting them up in a corner with snacks and crayons while I scrubbed bathrooms and changed linens.

It wasn't glamorous. But it was ours. A messy kind of progress, stitched together with love, survival, and a deep determination to keep going.

School.

Work.

Hope.

They didn't come easily.

Nothing ever had.

But for the first time in years, I wasn't just surviving.

I was building.

One step.

One breath.

One class at a time.

Balancing it all wasn't easy, but strangely enough, college felt simpler than the job—at least once I figured out where everything was located.

The community college sat nestled among twisting juniper trees, their branches reaching skyward like silent sentinels. The air smelled of sunbaked earth and sagebrush—wild, still, rugged, and calm all at once.

At 3,642 feet in elevation, the climb from the parking lot to the classrooms felt like a journey in itself. Some mornings, as I carried my books, the thinness of the air pressed against my lungs—a quiet reminder that I was somewhere new. Not just in geography. But in life.I hadn't walked these kinds of paths in years—not these literal paths, and certainly not ones paved with possibility.

And yet, here I was.

Doing it.

Finally earning my high school diploma.

The Weight I Carried

Coming out of 3L, I carried more than a schedule and a stack of used textbooks.

I carried grief.

Trauma.

The quiet ache of isolation.

And while I had made progress, healing wasn't linear.

I was still learning how to walk through the world again without bracing for impact.

Every interaction felt like a test I hadn't studied for.

Every hallway, every classroom held the possibility of both discovery and doubt.

I didn't know where I was headed yet—or even what I hoped it would become.

All I knew was that I was trying.

Trying to belong.

Trying to move forward.

Trying to build something from the pieces I still held in my hands.

Back Row Beginnings

My first class was English.

I remember walking in early, heart pounding, scanning the room for the least conspicuous seat—and making a beeline for the back row.

It felt safer there, tucked behind a sea of fresh-faced students who looked like they had just left high school—because most of them had.

They moved with a carefree ease, chatting easily, unburdened.

Their backpacks looked new.

Their notebooks uncreased.

Their faces free of the kind of weight I carried on my shoulders.

I felt like a foreigner in their world.

Older.

Wiser, maybe.

But also more unsure.

I clutched a plain spiral notebook—the kind you buy in a three-pack during back-to-school sales.

My pen was cheap.

My nerves were not.

My textbooks were all used—dog-eared, highlighted, and underlined by students who came before me. Some pages barely hanging on.

But they were mine.

Bought with a small work-study check that barely stretched far enough.

Still, I was grateful.

Grateful to be here.

Grateful for a second chance.

Every day, I returned to that back row and listened.

Took notes.

Scribbled margins full of wonder and worry.

Essays.

Discussions.

Analysis.

I hadn't done this in years, but something inside me flickered back to life.

I liked it here.

The words.

The stories.

The sense of possibility.

Learning (and Laughing) in the Dean's Office

That first morning, I stopped by the dean's office to introduce myself before class. Since I'd be working there immediately after, the secretary offered to hold my heavy books.

"You'll be needing them later," she said with a knowing smile.

I nodded, grateful. My arms would thank me later.

The dean's office felt grander than I expected—lined with dark wood shelves, thick leather-bound volumes, and the rich scent of paper and polish.

Along one wall, a fax machine, push-button phone, typewriter, and copy machine stood proudly in a row—like relics arranged by decade.

After a quick tutorial, I was left alone.

A Crash Course in "New" Technology

The phones rang. I rushed to answer. And promptly hung up on the first caller.

Panic surged.

I tried again—and transferred them to nowhere. My hands were sweaty. My cheeks burned.

Finally, after a few more fumbled attempts, I picked up and said brightly, "Dean's office, how can I help?"

Silence. Then: "Uh... I think I was just disconnected?"

I closed my eyes and stifled a laugh.

"Yes," I said. "That was me."

When I finally transferred the call correctly, I exhaled and rested my forehead in my palm.

It was the kind of stress you laugh about later—and maybe a little in the moment.

Thankfully, the dean's door stayed shut. And by the next call, I almost sounded like I knew what I was doing.

Finding My Place in the Classroom

Despite my nerves, I was surprised by how comfortable I felt sitting in a classroom again. I hadn't realized how much I missed learning—how good it felt to be in a space where ideas were shared like treasure.

Library Skills class, however? A different story.

It was mandatory. And tedious.

Sorting book after book, navigating outdated catalog systems—necessary, but soul-numbing.

Still, I did what was required.

Because finishing mattered more than comfort.

At first, I was unsure. Wondering if I really belonged.

But within days, that awkwardness began to fade. Confidence crept in.

The students were younger, yes—but instead of feeling out of place, I started to see the gift in that.

They reminded me it's never too late.

That even after years of detours, a path can still be picked up.

You Look Like You Belong

One day, something unexpected happened. A fellow student, closer to my age, stopped me in the hallway.

"Are you an attorney?" he asked, brow furrowed in curiosity.

I blinked. "What?"

He repeated it. "Are you an attorney?"

I looked down—beige linen pants, a long-sleeve pullover. Simple, but put-together.

And for the first time in a long time, I realized: I looked like someone who belonged.

I let out a soft laugh.

"No," I said. "I'm not."

But as I walked away, something shifted inside me.

He hadn't seen someone who never finished high school.

He hadn't seen someone who had spent weeks in a psychiatric ward.

He saw a woman who carried herself with quiet strength.

Someone who looked like she had a place in the world.

And that day, I walked the halls a little taller. A little more assured.

I wasn't just taking back what had been lost. I wasn't just earning credits.

I was showing up for the woman who had survived a courtroom, a hospital, and a thousand sleepless nights.

This time, I wasn't Ellen clinging to survival.

I was becoming someone new—someone I hadn't fully met yet.

Someone stronger.

Someone who would one day have a name of her own.

Chapter 52
Trust the Ride

Every day, when the weather allowed, I bundled up in my thickest coat, pulled a hat over my ears, and set out walking.

It wasn't about exercise.

It wasn't even about fresh air.

It was about movement—reminding myself, step by step, that I was still alive.

Still trying.

Still here.

As I walked, I spoke my mantra out loud into the open air:

"Every day I get better, better and better."

Not fancy.

Not poetic.

Just true.

I said it when my heart hurt.

When my legs ached.

Even when I wasn't sure I believed it.

Some days, the only thing I accomplished was putting one foot in front of the other and whispering those six words.

But still—I spoke it.

I walked it.

I lived it.

One frozen step at a time.

One whispered hope at a time.

Letting Go (Even Just a Little)

For as long as I could remember, I had avoided enclosed spaces.

Car washes.

Enclosed rides at fairs.

Any place where I didn't control the doors.

The fear was irrational, but real.

It wasn't just about claustrophobia—it was about control.

And letting go of control had never come easily.

One afternoon, the girls and I went to a small theme park called The Enchanted Garden.

The day was bright, the air crisp with spring.

They darted excitedly between attractions, their laughter chasing them down winding paths.

Then they begged me to go on an enclosed ride.

It wasn't a roller coaster.

Just a gentle, bobbing log ride—gliding through a man-made creek, floating up soft hills, winding through a shady tunnel.

Still, my stomach clenched at the entrance.

Old fear flared, warning me to stay on solid ground.

But their faces were so full of trust.

So full of hope.

I took a deep breath.

And I stepped into the log.

The ride jolted forward.

We drifted into the dim tunnel, cool water lapping around us, and I tightened my grip on the sides of the boat.

At first, all I could hear was the blood pounding in my ears.

But then—the laughter.

The wonder.

The sheer delight of my girls as we bobbed through the enchanted "garden."

I smiled.

Loosened my grip.

And for the first time in a long time,

I let myself float.

Not steer.

Not brace.

Just trust the ride.

The Car Wash (and Cheering Squad)

Not long after, we needed to wash the car.

Usually, I would have done it by hand—avoiding the mechanical tunnel of the automatic car wash at all costs.

But that day—maybe because of The Enchanted Garden, maybe because of the walking, maybe because of the mantra—I decided to try.

The girls were excited in the back seat.

"You can do it, Mom!"

"You're brave!"

"You're awesome!"

I pulled into the lane with shaking hands, heart racing.

As the rollers whooshed and brushes slapped the car, I squeezed the steering wheel and fought the urge to bolt.

But my girls clapped and whooped—cheering louder as the water sprayed and rainbow-colored soap splattered across the windshield.

Through their eyes, I wasn't trapped. I wasn't broken.

I was a hero in a car wash.

When we emerged back into daylight, dripping clean, I let out a breathless laugh.

They cheered again.

And I realized: I hadn't just washed the car. I had washed away a little fear, too.

The Mirror Exercise

Healing didn't come in giant leaps.

It came in a thousand small moments, stacked together.

One of the hardest things my counselor ever asked me to do was deceptively simple:

'Look into the mirror and say, "I like who you are becoming."'

The first time I tried, I couldn't even hold my own gaze.

The words felt foreign. Almost mocking.

But I kept trying.

Every day, even when it felt ridiculous, I stood in front of the mirror—staring into eyes that had seen too much sorrow—and said it anyway.

"I like who you are becoming."

At first, it was mechanical.

Then awkward.

Then one morning, I said it—and something inside me softened.

I meant it.

Not perfectly.

Not completely.

But enough.

Enough to believe there was something good growing inside me.

Enough to believe I was worth cheering for, too.

I was walking.

I was riding.

I was trusting.

I was speaking kindness to myself.

I wasn't just surviving anymore.

I was becoming someone new.

The classroom gave me confidence.

But healing?

Healing came on sidewalks.

In car washes.

In quiet moments when I dared to believe change was possible.

It came with motion, with mantras, with learning how to trust the ride—even when I couldn't see where it was going.

Chapter 53
The Ceremony That Mattered

There was no cap and gown.

No rows of folding chairs.

No stage to walk across.

No name announced over a microphone.

There was no formal ceremony.

But some victories don't need microphones.

They speak for themselves.

My high school diploma sat quietly in the dean's office, waiting with a stack of others. I came in, signed my name, and that was that.

No applause.

No tassel turn.

Just a quiet transaction of paper and pride.

But for me, it meant everything.

I had finished.

I walked out of the dean's office, smiling.

After all I had been through—the hospital, the healing, the rebuilding—I had done it. I had officially graduated from high school.

Not in the way most people do.

But in the way I needed to.

Quietly.

Privately.

Powerfully.

Still, I'd be lying if I said I didn't think about what I had missed.

No senior pictures.

No last-day-of-school rituals.

No walking across the stage with my class.

No arms around best friends, tossing caps into the air.

I had watched others go off to college, choose their majors, pick their dorm rooms—choose their life paths.

While mine... had taken a turn I hadn't seen coming.

That part hurt.

It still does sometimes.

But the moment I held that diploma in my hand, I knew this chapter was mine.

And then, something beautiful happened.

Leah surprised me with a graduation celebration.

It was at a very nice restaurant—one of those places with soft lighting and crisp tablecloths, where the food is plated like art and the laughter echoes gently off the walls.

All three of my daughters were there.

That alone would've been enough.

But Leah had done more.

She had made sure there was a cake—a full sheet cake, frosted in white with delicate yellow edging. In the center, done completely in icing, was a black cap and gown.

The cap had a red tassel, and piped across the top in yellow frosting was one word:

Congratulations.

It was perfect.

Not because it was grand or flashy.

But because it was thoughtful.

Because Leah saw me.

Saw the battles no one clapped for.

Saw the victories that were never photographed.

Because she celebrated the thing that had once felt so far out of reach.

I remember sitting at that table, surrounded by people who had stood with me through the worst of it.

My daughters beside me.

Leah smiling from across the table, her pride unmistakable.

There was no podium, no ceremony.

But this was my graduation.

And in many ways, it meant more than the traditional kind ever could.

Because I had earned every inch of that moment.

Because I wasn't just receiving a diploma.

I was reclaiming my life.

And the best part?

My girls were there to see it.

They saw their mom complete something hard.

They saw what healing looked like—not just in recovery, but in rising.

That night, as we laughed over dinner and cut into the cake, I didn't feel the absence of a stage or a speech.

I felt something better.

Whole.

Seen.

Proud.

Loved.

And that was the ceremony that mattered most.

The ceremony of rising.

Of being seen.

Of finally seeing myself.

Chapter 54
Becoming Lennie

After graduation, life didn't slow down.

It shifted.

Subtly at first—then all at once.

I had left Mexicali behind and stepped into a full-time job with a local real estate company. The work was steady and structured. Property management wasn't glamorous, but it came with a desk, a title, and a predictable paycheck—something I hadn't known in years.

And that's where Lennie began.

It started like most things do—quietly.

My new boss moved fast. Short emails. Short sentences. And without asking, she started changing my name too.

First, it showed up on inter-office memos.

Then voicemail messages.

Then—business cards.

At first, I didn't correct her.

And one day, I realized:

I didn't mind it.

I liked it.

Ellen had survived.

Ellen had fought and flailed and fumbled her way through grief, depression, and motherhood.

Ellen had held the pain, carried the silence, signed the hospital forms.

But Lennie?

Lennie was showing up to work in clean lines and fresh confidence.

Lennie wore black heels and soft blouses and held eye contact.

Lennie wasn't pretending anymore.

She was here.

For real.

For good.

The Name That Stuck

I started signing emails that way.

Lennie.

Not a nickname.

Not a phase.

It was mine.

And somehow, naming myself helped me own myself.

I was no longer defined by what I had survived—but by what I was choosing.

But I wasn't the same.

I was beginning to live with intention.

To speak with clarity.

To walk into rooms like I belonged.

And I did.

The Quiet Strength of Starting Over

At the office, I managed a small portfolio of properties—single-family homes, duplexes, the occasional fourplex. I returned tenant calls, dealt with complaints, filled out paperwork, and learned how to navigate demanding owners with practiced calm.

But the job wasn't just steady—it was fun.

Maxine, who ran the property management division, was a burst of energy in every room.

Lively, fast-talking, and always fun, she made even the most mundane tasks feel entertaining. I adored her.

We'd laugh over tenant stories, shake our heads at leaky roofs, and eat lunch together in the break room like old friends.

She believed in me.

From day one.

She didn't know about my past.

She cared that I showed up. That I could think on my feet. That I got the job done.

And I did.

I wasn't just managing properties.

I was managing to find my place.

One afternoon, I was showing a rental to a young couple. The house had a Dutch door in the back—split in the middle, with the top half swinging open to a snow-covered yard.

As I opened it for them, my hand paused on the latch.

It was the same kind of door.

And suddenly, I was back in a different winter—Years earlier.

Dean had just dropped the girls off after a weekend with him. They were inside the house, and I was at the Dutch door, gently closing the top half when he made one of his usual snide remarks—quiet enough to sting, loud enough to leave a mark.

I froze for a second.

Then I had called his name.

He turned around, smug and waiting.

And I said it.

Clear. Calm. Measured.

"Fuck you."

Then I had slammed the top half shut and bolted the lock.

That memory landed hard, a reminder: I had been finding my voice back then.

Not because it was funny.

But because it was done.

I stood up from my desk, smiled, and said, 'Right here.'

It was the smallest moment, but something in me clicked.

And now, standing here as a property manager, opening the same kind of door for a completely different reason, I smiled.

I had moved on.

I had become an entirely different person. Someone I liked.

From Paper to Presence

I still remember the day someone came into the office and asked for "Ellen."

Our receptionist tilted her head, confused.

"You mean Lennie?"

I stood up from my desk, smiled, and said,

"Right here."

It was the smallest moment.

But something in me clicked.

It wasn't just about the name.

It was about who I had become.

Someone no longer ashamed of her scars.

Someone who showed up even when she was afraid.

Someone who didn't need to explain the name or the story behind it—because it fit.

Not perfectly.

Not permanently.

But truthfully.

And that was more than enough.

Stepping Forward

I had found my name.

I had found my footing.

What I didn't know yet was that I was about to find something else—
A new kind of confidence.

A business that would push me past every limit I had set for myself.

And heels.

I had been someone who had lived in HUD housing wearing tennis shoes and was now standing in high heels, holding a microphone, and telling a room full of strangers how I got there.

But that's the next chapter.

Chapter 55
From HUD to High Heels

The cover of the company's magazine said it all:
"Learn How a Single Mom of Three from HUD Housing Makes Over $20,000 a Month."

That single mom was me.

I remember staring at that cover, half laughing, half crying—because if you'd told me just a few years earlier, when I was scraping change for groceries and hiding overdue bills, that I'd be featured in a national sales magazine, I would've thought you were nuts.

But here I was.

I had joined a sales company—and climbed all the way to the top.

Along the way, I didn't just learn how to sell a product.

I learned how to stand up straight, look someone in the eye, and believe I had something worth saying.

In the beginning, though? I was a total dweeb.

No college degree. No polished pitch. Not even a decent wardrobe.

Just a mama on a mission with a borrowed blazer and a heart full of shaky hope.

I'll never forget one of my first meetings—I showed up in leggings and a big pink sweater that practically swallowed me whole. At the time, I thought I looked put together.

Lorraine, a new team member I instantly clicked with, gently let me know what a sight I was in those early days.

We laughed about it for years.

And then there was one of my earliest presentations.

It was nighttime. Dark. Snow crusted the ground. I was scheduled to meet with a group of schoolteachers curious about the products. I was nervous, underdressed for the weather, and just trying to look the part.

I remember stepping out into the cold—wind slicing through my coat—walking toward the front door with my product bag in one hand and my confidence barely zipped up.

What I didn't realize—until it was too late—was that I'd grabbed my dark blue eyeliner pencil instead of my red lipliner. Out of habit, I had carefully outlined my lips before heading inside.

Yes.

Blue.

Lips.

I gave that entire presentation like I knew what I was doing—with navy blue lips smiling brightly under fluorescent lights. I answered questions. I took orders. I made eye contact.

I crushed it.

It wasn't until the very end—when I absentmindedly touched my mouth and saw the color smudged on my fingertip—that it hit me.

Blue.

I stared for a second in horror—then burst out laughing.

"It's a new shade," I said, grinning. "Just came out."

The teachers howled. They couldn't believe I hadn't noticed.

Honestly? Neither could I. But I had been so focused on showing up, I hadn't looked twice.

Later, my team surprised me with a group photo—every one of them wearing blue liner around their lips. I kept that picture for years.

Because that version of me deserved to be remembered.

The girl who showed up in the cold, got it wrong, and kept smiling anyway.

I was so green, I didn't even know if the business model was real.

I actually went to the city library to look it up—flipping through books and articles like I was investigating a secret society.

From HUD housing to fact-checking an entire industry.

I still laugh about it. But back then, people acted like it was some shady underground scheme. I wasn't about to put my name—or my hope—on the line without doing a little digging.

Once I realized the company was legit—and that I was actually good at it—I hit the ground running.

I started selling to anyone who'd listen: doctors' wives, nurses, accountants, stockbrokers.

I was slinging product out of the trunk of my car like a woman on a mission.

I'd laugh with clients in downtown parking lots, joking that we looked like we were doing something illegal. I'd pop the trunk, mix the product with a water bottle, and hand it over with a smile and a little pitch.

It was grassroots, gritty, and honestly? Kind of fun.

I built a business one car trunk and conversation at a time.

And before I knew it, I wasn't just surviving—I was thriving.

After my first year, something wild happened—my check jumped to over $10,000 in a single month.

I remember walking into the bank to deposit it, my hands literally shaking. I drove there slowly, like I had a trunk full of cash, checking the rearview mirror as if someone might be tailing me.

When I handed it to the teller, our eyes met—and I saw it.

That little flicker of surprise. Of recognition.

She didn't say anything.

But I could tell she knew:

This wasn't just a deposit.

It was a milestone.

And I couldn't stop grinning.

I didn't have a fancy degree or special credentials. I didn't even have a real office.

But I had every scar, every story, every scrap of resilience that had shaped me.

I had the gift of gab—and I was born with that. I could talk to anyone, anywhere, about anything.

And when I believed in something? Forget it. I was unstoppable.

I was the girl who took things one step at a time. Who didn't blink at "no."

Who had learned how to climb—not just mountains, but out of hospital beds and heartbreak.

That's what built my business.

Not scripts. Not strategy.

Just real conversations with real people.

I showed up with a trunk full of product and a whole lot of heart—and it turns out, that was more than enough.

The company took notice. One day a film crew arrived to feature me in a promotional video.

I was supposed to say, "I now earn a six-figure income."

Easy, right?

Except I kept saying, "I earn a six income figure."

Retake after retake. I had the lashes, the heels, the script—but my nerves wouldn't cooperate.

By the tenth take, we were all laughing so hard, the cameraman nearly dropped his gear.

But I didn't care.

I had arrived.

I was being filmed as a success story—and all without a degree, without connections, and definitely without a clue how to speak on camera.

Success didn't just change my income.

It changed how I saw myself.

I went from clearance racks out of desperation to choosing outfits that made me feel like a woman again.

One time, the airlines lost Lorraine's and my luggage right before a big conference.

Instead of crying, we looked at each other and said, "Let's go shopping."

We marched into the mall like two women on a mission—tried everything on, said yes to whatever we wanted, and walked out with new outfits, new makeup, and new underwear.

We strutted into that first session a little late, a little wild-eyed, and absolutely fabulous—just in time to take the stage as featured speakers.

And long before that, on my very first incentive trip—the one I had worked so hard to earn—I was racing through the airport in the rain, heels clicking, heart pounding.

As I dashed across the street, my overstuffed suitcase burst open right there on the curb.

Bras, business cards, and backup pantyhose flew everywhere.

I scrambled, laughing and mortified, trying to gather my life off the pavement.

I made that flight.

I made that trip.

And despite the grand entrance, I felt like I belonged.

Bermuda was my first big win.

And it was beautiful.

There was another time, at a huge convention, when the company's founder told the men,

"You guys need to start making enough to buy your wives diamonds."

A few minutes later, the spotlight hit me as I walked onstage.

I looked out at the crowd, held up both hands, and said:

"This girl doesn't need a man—she buys her own diamonds."

The roar of the room echoed in my chest.

I had gone from whispering in the back row to owning the stage.

Here's what I want to say about that chapter of my life:

Behind the cheesy slogans and overused hashtags, this was where I learned to believe in myself again.

It gave me a voice, a tribe, and a chance to rewrite my story—not just as a survivor, but as a leader.

It wasn't about vitamins or skin cream.

It was about realizing that my life didn't have to stay small just because it started that way. I wasn't just paying bills anymore.

I was building confidence.

Raising three daughters.

Showing them what was possible.

I was becoming someone who no longer apologized for taking up space.

I had found my voice in front of rooms filled with strangers.

Funny enough, somewhere along the way, that fear I once had—the one that sent me to the doctor convinced I had cancer because I could feel a lump every time I sat down?

It disappeared.

I knew exactly what it was now.

It was my tailbone.

And it wasn't sticking out from being too thin anymore.

My weight was healthy.

My body was strong.

I was no longer wasting away—I was rooted. Grounded.

And if I felt that little bump when I slid into the driver's seat?

I just smiled.

That's my reminder.

Not of how fragile I once was—but of how far I've come.

Because that's how life works sometimes.

You climb out of HUD housing.

You learn to walk in heels.

You become the woman who buys her own diamonds.

Chapter 56
Finding the Right Fit

By the time I was making a six-figure income, I had built something solid—both on paper and inside myself.

I had confidence.

I had heels.

I had daughters who looked at me with pride.

And now, for the first time in years, I wasn't afraid of starting over—even in love.

Dating in your late 30s is like rummaging through a thrift store. Sometimes you find a gem. Most of the time, you leave with something that smells funny and doesn't fit.

I used to tell people: "I'm just trying on shoes—just looking for a pair that fits and feels comfortable."

Let's just say... I tried on a lot of shoes.

Because healing meant putting myself out there.

Laughing again.

Risking a little heartache in exchange for hope.

Because maybe, just maybe—The right fit wasn't something you chase.

It was something that found you when you were finally ready.

I didn't know it then, but the right fit was just a few years down the road.

First, though... these.

The Pool Boy — The Flashy Flip-Flop

Looked good poolside but had zero support in real life.

Met him swimming. Lifeguard. Tall, tan, overconfident.

One day at the grocery store, he ran down the aisle, threw me over his shoulder like a rom-com scene. People stared. I laughed. Sort of.

Two days later, he stormed into my college classroom yelling, "Roses for Lennie! Roses for Lennie!" laying them dramatically on my desk.

I sank into my seat and whispered, "Oh my gawd... Next."

The Hairdresser — The Silent Slip-On

Looked like a good fit... until I realized there was no conversation whatsoever.

He did hair. Talked to women all day. I figured, great communicator. Wrong.

I asked questions. Smiled. Filled the silence. He... nodded.

"Saving your words for later?" I asked. He shrugged.

Next.

The Felon — The Untied Work Boot

Looked sturdy. Super handsome. Good with kids. Came with baggage.

A good friend introduced us.

After a few months:

"There's something I should probably tell you... I'm a felon."

I nodded. Internally screamed.

Next.

The Dentist — The Polished Custom Orthotic

Looked like he was built for long-term support—clean-cut, steady, professional.

But twelve dates in, he leaned across the table, smiled, and said:

"You were almost the one."

Almost?

Like a crown that didn't quite fit.

I wasn't looking for almost.

I wanted permanent, not temporary.

Next.

The Double-Dipper — The Loafer with Hidden Laces

Reliable fit... until I found out he was walking in two households.

At a nail salon, the chatty tech asked about my boyfriend. I answered.

"That must be a big company," she said. "My best friend is dating someone from there... same name."

Stomach. Dropped.

Packed up his leather coat, portable TV, and a few other belongings. Tossed them on the deck, in the rain.

Next.

The Harley Guy — The Worn-In Leather Boot

Sexy in theory. Felt great—until the sole gave out.

Ten years younger. Harley rider. Freedom and hair blowing in the wind.

Until I realized he brought excuses, not a future. Wanted me to support him.

Next.

The Pretty Boy — The Shiny Designer Loafer

Fifteen years younger. So fun. Looked amazing.

Until a hostess pointed at him and said, "Your son is sitting right over there."

I nearly evaporated.

Lovely dinner.

Next.

The Professor — The Stiff Dress Shoe

Credentials: solid.

Personality: missing.

When my daughters asked him, "What are your intentions with our mom?" he broke into a nervous sweat.

Didn't matter. He bored me to sleep.

Next.

The Blue Light Special — The Clearance Rack Mystery Shoe

Silent. Mysterious. Off.

Manager at Kmart. Nicknamed "The Blue Light Special."

At my Christmas party, my 75-year-old aunt stood behind him, slicing her finger dramatically across her throat: absolutely not.

Message received.

Next.

The Ex-Talker – The Loafer Stuck in the Past

He walked into Margarita's like he was auditioning for a tequila commercial—smooth, confident, just the right amount of stubble.

We hit it off. He asked me out. Took me to great restaurants. Planned fun dates.

But by the third date and second appetizer, I realized I wasn't on a date.

I was in a support group—for him.

Every conversation circled back to her—his ex.

How they met. How she left. How misunderstood he still was.

I sipped my drink. Nodded politely. Mentally built a raft to float away on.

By dessert, I knew her middle name, her shoe size, and what kind of salad dressing she preferred.

I didn't even know his last name.

He paused once and asked, "Am I talking about her too much?"

I smiled.

"Only if you weren't hoping for another date."

Next.

The Grounded Narcissist – The Patent Leather Pilot

He sold high-end homes and claimed to fly private planes—though the only time I saw him near one was in a suspiciously cropped photo.

He was always standing next to the plane, never in it.

Like a guy who takes selfies beside a yacht at a marina and calls it "his."

His shoes were glossy Italian leather. His hair? Overstyled. His conversation? Mostly about himself.

He once told me, "Being a pilot is a mindset."

So is being full of it.

He listed his accomplishments like I was filling out a loan application.

"Women my age usually can't keep up," he said with a wink.

I smiled and thought, "Good thing I'm not trying to keep up. I'm trying to get out."

And I did.

But not before he came storming out of the house as I backed out of the driveway, yelling,

"No one ever leaves me!"

I rolled down the window.

"Congratulations," I said. "Today's your first."

Then I drove off without looking back.

The seatbelt sign was on.

And this girl was cleared for takeoff.

Next.

Except... there were no more nexts.

Because he was the last one I ever had to say that to.

The final "Next."

After him, I didn't need to try on any more shoes.

I was done shopping.

Done shrinking.

Done mistaking polish for substance.

And somewhere beyond that runway...

The right fit was waiting.

Here's the truth:

My daughters were always right.

They saw the wrong pair of shoes coming every time.

After all the mismatched shoes, half-hearted conversations, and dramatic exits, I had stopped looking.

I wasn't bitter—just tired.

I had a full life.

A career that gave me confidence.

Daughters who reminded me daily that I didn't need to settle.

And with each "Next," I had gotten clearer about what I deserved—not just in love, but in life.

I wasn't waiting for someone to save me anymore.

I was learning to stand tall, speak up, and step forward in my own heels.

And soon, those heels would carry me somewhere I never expected—onto a stage, into a spotlight, and straight into a whole new fit.

Chapter 57
An Email & A Ski Trip

L orraine and I were in her home office, doing what we did best—
running a business, running our mouths, and running on candy.

We were both making six-figure incomes by then—two women who had climbed from survival to success, side by side. Her desk was covered in color-coded folders. Mine? Sticky notes.

Everywhere. If Lorraine ever reads this, she'll laugh out loud at the memory—her tidy systems drowning in my rainbow storm of Post-its.

We wore sweatpants, T-shirts, and zero apologies. And we didn't just sip tea—we devoured French fries while planning our next wave of training calls.

"Snack?" I asked, tossing a piece of licorice across the desk.

She caught it midair without missing a beat. "Only if you try one of my new sour gummies."

I groaned. "Those things should come with a warning label."

She grinned. "Builds character."

We didn't just build businesses together—we built a friendship that changed both our lives.

When we first met, we were strangers. But after countless hours of laughter, late-night prep sessions, pep talks, and PowerPoints—we became best friends. We held trainings together, traveled together, rolled up our sleeves together. We didn't inherit success—we earned it. And we celebrated the hell out of it, too.

Our first big win together was Bermuda. The company flew us out for an all-expense-paid incentive trip.

On our third day, we rented mopeds and set off to explore.

I took the lead. Bold, confident, feeling like a boss. What I forgot? Bermuda drives on the opposite side of the road.

I turned right out of the lot like a mighty leader—only to find a bus barreling straight toward me.

My friends screamed, I screamed—the sheer chaos. It was terrifying and hilarious all at once. I yanked the handlebars and veered off just in time, landing somewhere between a bush and a life lesson.

Lorraine and I laughed about that for years.

There were so many trips like that. Warm climates. Poolside drinks. Dinner parties where we got to wear dresses that hadn't come from the clearance rack. But what meant the most was always the same: our friendship. Sharing the joy. The absurdity. The victories.

Her husband joined us on every trip. They were a team—steady, funny, fiercely loyal to each other. Watching them together reminded me that good love existed, even if I hadn't found it yet.

I hadn't expected to find this kind of joy. This kind of partnership. Not just in business, but in life.

And that's exactly where I was—laughing in sweatpants, sorting candy and color-coded schedules with my best friend—when the email arrived.

The Email That Started It All

I clicked the notification without thinking—then stopped breathing for a second.

"I heard you are going downhill skiing this coming weekend and wondered if you wanted some company."

Signed,
Doug.

Doug?

I stared. Blinked. Read it again.

Then I turned the screen toward Lorraine.

"I can't get a guy to walk across the room to ask me out," I said, "and this one wants to fly 2,400 miles for a ski weekend."

Her chair squeaked as she scooted closer. "Who is Doug?"

"He's a friend of my sister and brother-in-law. Someone they've known for years—flies out every month for business. I think they even go salmon fishing together in the fall when he's in town."

Lorraine narrowed her eyes at the screen, scrutinizing every word.

"He wants to go skiing with you next weekend?" she asked, her voice dipping into suspicion.

I tapped my chin, pretending to be deep in thought. "This is a setup," I said, grinning.

"A setup?" she asked, already catching on.

"Yes! No one knows I'm planning on skiing alone next weekend except..."

We said it at the same time. "Alice and George!"

I laughed. My sister had been meddling.

Lorraine folded her arms. "So what are you going to say?"

I placed my fingers on the keyboard, smiling. "I'm going to say this..."

The Novice-on-the-Snow Act

I typed quickly: "I need to warn you I am not very good on the snow."
That was a complete lie.

Not only had I taken lessons in high school—I'd been on the ski team both sophomore and junior year. I wasn't just comfortable on the slopes—I was good. I lived in ski country now, with some of the best powder in the state. Skiing was second nature to me.

But I wasn't about to let Doug know that. Not yet.

Doug replied almost instantly.

I smirked and kept typing:

"A week will give me time to lose 40 pounds and have my teeth straightened."

His response came just as fast:

"Same here. I'll try to grow a few inches, tame my hair, and get my braces taken off. Let's both aim high."

I laughed out loud, caught off guard by his humor.

Maybe he wasn't as buttoned-up and serious as I'd assumed.

Confidence, Sales, and Saying Yes to New Adventures

As I stared at the screen, fingers hovering above the keyboard, I felt something different—something I wouldn't have felt a few years earlier.

I had spent years building myself back up, proving I was capable and strong. Sales hadn't just given me a career—it had taught me how to own my confidence. How to take risks. How to trust my instincts.

Would I have said yes to this ski trip five years ago? Probably not.

But now?

350

Now, I was in a place where I embraced opportunities instead of hiding from them. Now, I saw this email not as a risk—but as a new kind of adventure.

I leaned back in my chair, remembering that Christmas party—how Doug had barely spoken to me, how polished he seemed. And now, here he was—flying across the country to go skiing with me.

I glanced at Lorraine, who was still watching me expectantly.

"This will be an adventure," I told her, grinning as I hit send.

And if nothing else—I was going to make sure he believed every word of my "novice on the snow" act. At least for a little while.

Not out of fear.

But for the fun of it.

For the first time in years, I wasn't bracing for pain.

I was letting myself enjoy the spark.

And that, too, was healing.

Chapter 58
This Shoe Fit

I spent very little time thinking about work over the next five days. My heart already knew something was about to change—even if my mind hadn't caught up yet.

I was excited. Nervous. Intrigued.

I called my sister, not bothering with small talk.

"Okay, I know you're behind Doug emailing me!"

She didn't even try to deny it.

"Yes," she admitted, not missing a beat. "We just thought you had a lot in common. He skis. You ski. He's single. You're single. He's a wonderful man."

I rolled my eyes. Probably too wonderful. Not my type.

But still... I was looking forward to it.

Prepping for the Ski Trip (Or So I Thought)

The anticipation built throughout the week.

I bought a new sweater, a new pair of jeans. December was cold, I told myself—I needed warm clothes. Never mind that nice ski gear already lined my closet.

I took my skis in to be cleaned and waxed, loving the thought of gliding through fresh powder.

The crisp mountain air, the sound of the chairlift, the rush of carving down the slopes—this was my happy place.

My friends and I had always been first on the lifts in the morning and the last ones off at the end of the day.

I hoped Doug was ready for us.

The Date Begins

As the day of Doug's flight arrived, anticipation and nerves fought for control.

Stay calm. Act natural.

It had been a long time since I had been on a date. And this wasn't just any date.

This was 2,400 miles different.

His plane landed right on time at our small airport. A few minutes later, my phone rang.

"I'm staying at the High Desert Inn. Can we meet there for dinner later tonight? Say 7:30? Do you know where that is?" Doug asked.

"Sure do."

I smiled, remembering my graduation dinner there—the surprise party Leah had planned, the cake with the cap and gown, the yellow piping and the word Congratulations across the top. That hotel held good memories.

"7:30 will be great," I told him.

All week, my sister had been calling to talk him up.

"He's kind, he's funny, he's brilliant."

"I'm sold, Sis. You should be in sales," I quipped, laughing.

But deep down, I was intrigued. Really intrigued.

Doug looked just as I remembered when I walked into the restaurant.

Tailored. Not a hair out of place.

That full head of jet-black hair, kind features, and an ease about him that instantly put me at ease too.

"Hi! I made it!" he said, flashing a warm smile and pulling out a chair across from him.

The conversation flowed effortlessly.

We talked about everything—our lives, our pasts, our favorite places to travel.

We were the last table to leave, long after the last round was called.

I felt comfortable. Listened to. Seen.

All the nervousness melted away, replaced by something I didn't quite have words for yet.

The Ski Trip That Wasn't

I had been on the mountain enough times to know how unpredictable the weather could be.

"Let me ask the waiters about tomorrow's ski conditions," I said, gesturing toward the staff.

"They work here, so they get free ski passes. They'll know what's going on up there."

I returned to the table with a distressed look on my face.

"A storm's blown in. Tomorrow will be a total whiteout. They're expecting 40-mile-per-hour winds or higher. The chairs won't be operating."

Doug shook his head, laughing.

"Guess we'll have to change plans."

The Brewery & The Moment That Changed Everything

We met for lunch the next day at a brewery instead of on the slopes.

The weather may have changed our plans, but it didn't change how easy it felt being with him.

We sat across from each other, sharing stories, laughing, enjoying the warmth of the fire inside while the storm raged outside.

At one point, mid-burger, Doug casually pinched between his fingers the small bulges on each side of his waist.

"Know what they call these?" he asked casually.

I stared at him, afraid to say what I was thinking.

"They are my sperm sacs," he said, giving each side a healthy squeeze.

I lost it.

The hamburger I had been chewing flew out of my mouth as I burst into laughter, utterly caught off guard.

For one breathless second, the whole world stilled.

Then our eyes met, and we were both laughing uncontrollably.

The kind of laughter that erases time, that makes everything else fade into the background.

That moment changed something.

It was real. It was genuine.

It was the moment I started to fall in love with this man.

The Kiss Before Goodbye

The storm never passed.

Doug and I never made it up to the slopes.

Instead, his last night in town came too quickly. The next morning, he would drive three hours across the pass to meet with my brother-in-law and his company before flying home.

We had spent two nights talking late into the night, conversation flowing as effortlessly as the laughter.

And now, it was time to say goodbye.

We stood in the cold winter air, our cars parked beside each other outside his hotel.

Instead of saying goodbye, Doug kept talking.

Jabbering.

Rambling about something—I don't even remember what.

I just sat there in the passenger seat of his rental car, watching him, waiting.

Finally, I couldn't take it anymore.

"Can you just shut up and kiss me?" I blurted.

Doug blinked. Stopped mid-sentence.

For one breathless second, the whole world stilled.

And then, he did.

The words didn't matter anymore.

The snow swirled around us, the storm still raging, but I barely noticed.

Because in that moment, I knew.

Doug wasn't as straight-laced as I once thought.

And I was falling in love.

As I drove home that night, snowflakes swirling in my headlights, I realized something had shifted.

Not just in the air—but in me.

This man had flown across the country in a snowstorm, and somehow, against all odds, it had felt easy.

Natural.

Undeniably real.

It wasn't just a date.

It was the beginning of something.

And somewhere deep down, I already knew—This one was different.

This shoe fit.

Chapter 59
The Road to Us

After that snowy weekend, Doug didn't let distance get in the way. He courted me from the other side of the country—flying in every weekend from Ohio to the Pacific Northwest. For nine months leading up to our wedding, I picked him up from the airport nearly every Friday night and took him back every Sunday. And every weekend, we had something planned.

Wineries.

Trips to the Oregon Coast.

Adventures in the high desert.

A different restaurant to try every time.

We even met up at ski resorts in Colorado when our schedules allowed. But Doug made the distance feel small—week after week.

He'd been traveling to the Pacific Northwest for thirteen years on business and knew the region well. Still, it all felt new when we were discovering it together.

Looking back, I'm not sure how we had that much energy. But we did.

And we loved every minute of it.

One weekend, we met up in Colorado. Some of Doug's family flew in from Florida to join us, and we all met at the Denver airport. They were warm, kind, and full of stories. I had heard a lot about them. They had heard plenty about me. I only hoped I could meet their expectations.

Evidently... I did.

One afternoon on the slopes, Doug's sister-in-law, Gail, skied up beside me around 2:00 p.m. and asked, "Wanna call it a day and go get some hot cocoa with a splash of mint schnapps?"

I grinned. "Of course."

We ditched the guys and cozied up with warm drinks, watching the snow fall from inside the lodge.

She turned to me, wide-eyed, and asked, "So... how do you like Doug?"

I didn't hesitate. "I like him a lot."

She smiled. And from that day on, Gail became more than family— she became a true friend.

We've traveled together ever since.

The Proposal

About three months into our long-distance weekends, Doug told me he had a day planned.

We went house shopping. Yep—house shopping.

At every stop, he'd ask what I thought.

Did I like the kitchen? The layout? The neighborhood?

I played along, telling him what I liked and didn't like...knowing the whole time—or at least thinking I knew—what he was eventually going to ask me.

Then we visited five wineries—each more beautiful than the last.

The mood was light, playful. But I could feel something building.

That evening, he took me to a gorgeous restaurant overlooking the river and the city skyline. The sun was setting. The lights of the city were beginning to glow.

And then—he leaned across the table and said,

"If a certain someone were to ask a certain someone a certain question... what would that certain someone's answer be?"

I smiled as he talked.

"Well," I said, "that certain someone would need to know the other certain someone's certain question before she could answer that certain question."

Doug laughed—a soft, nervous chuckle.

Then he asked, simply,

"Would you marry me?"

I laughed too—that warm, full kind of laugh that bubbles up when something just feels right.

"Yes," I said.

He looked almost surprised.

I grinned.

"I knew you were going to ask me."

"Really?" he asked.

"Doug, it's not every day a woman gets taken house shopping and winery hopping on the same date."

We laughed together—the kind of laughter that already felt like a lifetime in the making.

It was unexpected.

It was perfect.

It was us.

And it had all started with an email.

Years later, I came across a box tucked in a closet corner. Inside were the printed emails Doug and I had exchanged during the weekdays we were apart. He had saved every single one.

It was like flipping through love letters from a different life—funny, honest, sweet.

We sat together and read them aloud, laughing until our sides hurt.

A Wedding Among the Vines

Doug and I were intent on being married at a winery.

He had one request: a pastor to officiate.

What neither of us realized at the time was just how difficult it would be to find a pastor willing to marry us outside a traditional church setting—especially at a winery.

After many phone calls, we finally found someone: an 81-year-old pastor who agreed to officiate.

We met with him several times in the months leading up to the wedding to walk through the service—timing, vows, the flow of the day.

Then—exactly one week before the wedding—Doug and I sat with him for our final meeting.

We had gone through our checklist. We were confirming the details.

Everything was ready.

As we stood to leave his office, I smiled and said,

"See you next Saturday at 1:00 p.m."

What he said next sent a shockwave through me.

"Oh, I can't marry you next Saturday," he replied casually, gesturing toward a large calendar on the wall.

"I'll be at a conference in Seattle that day."

Doug and I froze.

Seriously??

Surely, we had misheard.

But no—he said it again, smiling faintly. Looking more frail than I had realized.

He said it like we had asked him to reschedule lunch, not cancel the most important day of our lives.

We were stunned. Speechless.

He had known the date for months.

Now, with just one week to go—we had no one to marry us.

Cue the scramble.

Dozens of phone calls. Voicemails. Dead ends.

We were nearly out of options—until, by some miracle, we reached a kind-hearted youth pastor who said yes.

Yes, to the winery.

Yes, to the celebration.

Yes, to us.

Doug and I stood on the deck of a winery, overlooking the most breathtaking view.

The sun hung low in the sky, casting a golden glow over the vineyards.

Rolling green hills stretched for miles, dusted in late-summer warmth and framed by clusters of trees and soft shadows.

The wooden deck creaked beneath our feet, worn smooth by years of celebration.

I wore a long navy-blue satin dress, fitted with delicate spaghetti straps and a sheer sheath overlay that shimmered softly in the light.

I held a bouquet of sweet blooms, their fragrance rising gently in the breeze.

My heart fluttered as I looked at Doug—so handsome in his black tuxedo, standing at the edge of the deck waiting for me.

I walked down the wooden steps toward him, each step echoing with memory, love, and the quiet certainty that this was where I was meant to be.

Both of my sisters stood beside me, radiant and smiling.

Both brothers were close by.

As I looked around the gathering, I saw Leah, Lorraine, Paula, and other lifelong friends there to celebrate with us—women who had walked beside me, laughed with me, cried with me.

Now they were here to witness this new beginning.

It wasn't just a wedding—It was a moment that felt like everything had led us here.

A Perfect Beginning

The morning air had been crisp and fresh, carrying the soft scent of grapevines as the sun began its slow ascent over the valley.

I had taken a deep breath, letting the moment settle in around me.

We were getting married in one of the most beautiful places I had ever seen.

And somehow, it felt just right.

All the roads.

All the struggles.

All the healing.

It had all brought me here.

To this beautiful place.

To this beautiful day.

To him.

The Moment That Made Us Laugh

As the pastor stood before us, his voice steady and warm,

He asked the familiar words:

"Who gives this woman to be married?"

Without hesitation, two voices rang out in unison.

"We do!"

I turned to see my uncle—the man who had stepped in as a father figure so many years ago—and my brother-in-law, George, the very person who had introduced Doug and me, standing side by side.

I laughed, my heart swelling at the sight of them—Two men who had supported me, protected me, guided me through some of the hardest years of my life—Now standing here, giving their blessing to my new beginning.

Doug squeezed my hand.

And in that moment, surrounded by love, family, and the sweeping beauty of the vineyards below, I knew...

This was exactly where I was meant to be.

The Wedding Night — A Cake & A Promise

Later that night, after the music, dancing, and laughter had ended, we finally relaxed in our chairs at the dining room table, kicking off our shoes.

Doug leaned back, a smile still playing on his lips.

"That was a great party!" he said, his voice full of contentment.

"Yes," I agreed, laughing softly, feeling the lingering joy from the day. "We did a good job putting it on!"

Then suddenly, I gasped.

"Wait—the wedding cake!" I jumped up, remembering the top tier we had brought home. "We need to put this in the freezer," I declared.

Doug stood up, helping me wrap it.

But as we started to carefully wrap each piece in cellophane, we both paused.

We looked at each other.

Then at the cake.

Then back at each other.

And without a word—without hesitation—We ditched the cellophane and stuffed the cake into our mouths,

Laughing as frosting smeared our fingers.

"To many happy years," Doug said, swallowing a bite. "I love you, Mrs. Campbell."

I smiled, my heart full.

"I love you, too, Mr. Campbell," I whispered, kissing him with frosting still on my lips.

We smiled, knowing there was a whole world out there to explore together.

Chapter 60
Gathering The Pieces

Embracing the Island Life

For many years, Doug and I built a wonderful life in the Pacific Northwest—a place filled with seasons, skiing, adventure, and cherished memories.

But when it came time to think about retirement,

The decision felt easy.

It wasn't just a move.

It was a homecoming.

Hawaii had already become a second home to us long before we ever moved.

Our middle daughter, Ann, and her husband, Nick, had moved there years earlier.

We found ourselves visiting often—babysitting, celebrating holidays, embracing the island life whenever we could.

With each visit, we fell deeper in love with the islands, the culture, and the sense of Aloha that surrounded us.

And then, when the time was right,

We knew—This was where we were meant to be.

Just one year after we made the move, another daughter and her significant other also chose Hawaii as home.

Now, We all live within five minutes of each other.

What started as a love for the islands had turned into a life surrounded by family, warmth, and the peaceful rhythm of the ocean.

We had built a life in the Pacific Northwest.

But Hawaii had been waiting for us all along.

And it was time to step fully into it.

These days, life moves slower—and sweeter.

Most mornings, Doug and I sit on the lanai together.

He sips his coffee. I make myself a matcha latte, just the way I like it.

We watch the sun rise over the palms, letting the light stretch slowly across the lawn.

The neighbor's cat sometimes wanders by.

The air smells like plumeria and red jasmine.

Sometimes we don't even speak—just breathe it in.

The stillness, the rhythm, the gift of this chapter in our lives.

Sometimes, one of the girls will stop by after work.

They leave their "slipas" at the door and step barefoot onto the lanai, greeting us with smiles and stories.

Often, we end up talking about our next trip—planning another staycation, an interisland getaway, or a big overseas adventure we'll take together.

And I look around, quietly amazed.

Not at the beauty of the island—though that's always there.

But at the fact that I get to be here.

Whole.

Held.

Home.

The Heart of Aloha

One evening, as Doug and I sat by the ocean, the waves gently lapping at the shore,

I let the warm water wash over my feet, the sand shifting softly beneath me.

The sun dipped lower on the horizon, painting the sky in hues of gold, orange, and lavender.

"You know, back when we first moved here," I said, watching as the sun slipped below the horizon.

"I thought success was about going faster, achieving more. But Hawaii taught me different. Life isn't about the rush—it's about experiencing every moment. It's about simply watching the sun rise and the sun set."

Doug nodded, his gaze thoughtful.

"Yes," he said. "In all the years I traveled, I never saw myself so relaxed... or playing the ukulele."

I smiled, because I loved it when he played.

"It's so relaxing, and I like being the entertainment," I teased.

Doug chuckled because sometimes, as he strummed, I danced my own version of the hula—Not gracefully, but with joy.

The kind of joy that doesn't need to be perfect to be real.

"Another thing I've really noticed," I continued, "is the way people respect their elders here, calling them 'Auntie' and 'Uncle.' I realized how deeply wisdom is valued. It's not just about age—it's about the experiences that shape us."

Doug nodded again, taking a sip from his thermos, the familiar sound of the waves filling the comfortable silence between us.

We sat there in the glow of twilight, the salty air brushing against our skin, the peaceful hum of the island settling in our bones.

Life had slowed down in all the best ways.

The Healing Calm of the Ocean

Another evening, the girls and I sat beside the ocean, waiting for the Sun to disappear into the horizon.

I smiled at my daughters, feeling so much love in that moment—a love that spanned generations, stretching from what was to what still is.

As the breeze touched my skin, a memory surfaced—one I rarely spoke of, but never truly forgot.

Years ago, I saw him again.

The man who had assaulted me.

He knew I was pregnant. He knew the baby was killed in a car accident.

Over the years, I had seen him from a distance—never close enough to speak. Just enough to feel the quiet knot tighten in my stomach.

But that day, at a funeral, he approached me.

Crying. Apologizing. Saying he was sorry.

I looked at him—just once.

Then I turned and walked away.

Not because I was afraid.

Not because I didn't have words.

But because I didn't need to speak;

That silence? That walk-away?

That was power.

And now, here I was—decades later—at the edge of the ocean, my daughters beside me, the sky painted in gold.

Whole. Steady. Free.

The Floating Lantern Festival

"Mom, you might be interested in the Japanese Floating Lantern Festival this year," Ann told me one afternoon.

"It's held every summer in August."

"Really? What's it all about?" I asked, intrigued.

"You create paper lanterns. The supplies are all donated—four sheets of paper placed on a wooden stand. On each sheet, you write a message, something you want to say to a loved one who has passed... something in their memory," she explained.

"At sunset, everyone sets their lantern on the water with a candle lit inside and watches as they all float together."

"It's really beautiful to watch," Ann added in her practical, matter-of-fact way.

I looked into her brown eyes as they searched my own, her brown hair lifting in a light breeze.

"That sounds wonderful," I said, amazed I hadn't heard of it before.

"Where is it held?"

"Fairmont Orchid, in the bay," Ann replied.

"As the lanterns are released into the bay, they take with them our healing prayers and written messages to honor and remember those who have passed," she added.

My heart absorbed her words.

"What an amazing ceremony to honor your loved ones," I whispered

I already knew exactly whose names I would write on my lantern.

The Floating Lantern Ceremony

Marie, Ann, and I sat at a small round table, just big enough for each of us to have space to lay our sheets of paper and write our messages.

The air held an earthy scent mixed with Hawaiian Jasmine, with a peaceful hush falling over the crowd.

I watched as Ann used a thin-tipped red Sharpie to create a design and followed suit.

"I like that," I said, admiring her creativity.

I set my colored pens on the table and began to write:

To Jonathan – My love is forever and always. ♥

To Mom – Love beyond measure. ♥

To Dad – Missing our starry nights together. ♥

I glanced at my daughters, loving the care and thoughtfulness they poured into their lanterns.

As my eyes drifted to Ann's paper, I saw her words:

"I would have loved to have met you."

She was writing to Jonathan.

Tears welled in my eyes.

Love reached across the spaces time could not erase.

We were all connected—then, now, always.

I smiled at my girls, feeling so much love in that moment—a love that spanned generations, reaching from what was to what still is.

Letting Go, Holding On

The almost-full moon cast its glow across the water, illuminating the tiny ripples on the ocean's surface.

The light reflected like diamonds dancing across the waves, shimmering with the rhythm of the tide.

I stood at the water's edge, the soft sand cool beneath my feet, holding the Japanese paper lantern I had carefully created.

The delicate frame felt light in my hands, yet its meaning was weighty—filled with memories, love, and gratitude.

As I set it gently onto the water, I watched as the night's gentle breeze carried it away, the small

flame flickering but steady.

I had spent so much of my life fighting, surviving, rebuilding.

And now, in this moment,

I simply existed in peace.

The lantern drifted farther out to sea,

a quiet messenger of my journey.

A journey that had brought me to right here, right now.

Living a life I never thought possible.

With lasting memories of those I loved tucked away in a special place within my heart—never to be forgotten.

I smiled, my heart full, as I watched my paper lantern sail farther into the night.

And as I stood there at the edge of the ocean, the waves brushing my ankles, I felt it—not just memory, not just release, but something holy.

These days, I don't need a church to know that God is within me.

I feel His presence when the breeze touches my face and whispers Aloha, when the sunset tosses orange and red across the sky, in a hibiscus bud just beginning to bloom, and beneath a canopy of stars that reminds me—His love was never conditional.

It was always here.

Always mine.

Even when I couldn't feel it.

Even when I didn't believe I was worthy of it.

Now I know:

God is love.

And love was never lost.

One afternoon while driving together here in Hawaii, Ann turned to me quietly and said, "You've been through so much pain and heartache, Mom. You are the strongest person I know."

She didn't say it dramatically. She just said it—and meant it.

I kept my eyes on the road, my hands on the wheel, but her words landed in my chest like something sacred.

I didn't need to explain anything. I didn't need to say a word.

In that moment, I saw myself through her eyes.

And I believed her.

The lantern drifted across the bay, its small flame still glowing.

And with it, a piece of me went too—grateful, open, whole.

Finally, I understood what it meant to come home.

Not just to a place.

But to myself.

To peace.

To love.

To light.

* * * *

If you're walking through grief...
you're not alone.
If you've been silenced...
your voice still waits.
If you've lost someone...
love still holds.
And even if you've lost yourself along the way—
you can still gather the pieces.

A Letter to the Girl Who Survived

You didn't know if you'd make it — and that's okay.

You learned to breathe through pain no one could see, to stand back up when no one noticed you'd fallen, to carry shattered pieces that didn't look like they could ever fit back together. But still, you kept going. You found your way forward, one fragile piece at a time.

There were days when silence felt safer than truth, when shame pressed heavier than grief. But even then, grace kept showing up — in a friend's voice, in your daughter's eyes, in the quiet beat of your own heart.

I wish I could sit beside you now. I'd take your hand and whisper: "You are not what happened to you. You are the one who gathered the pieces."

* * * *

To the one reading these pages:

If you've ever felt broken beyond repair... you are not alone.

If you've ever wondered whether healing is possible... it is.

If you've ever questioned whether your story matters...

I promise you, it does.

This book was never just about my past.

It's about what's possible when we stop hiding.

When we stop pretending.

When we finally say, "This happened — and I'm still here."

There are pieces I will always hold — and others I've set afloat in light and love.

I am not what was broken.

I am what survived.

And so are you.

With a full heart,

Lennie

Acknowledgments

This book would not exist without the people who lifted me, listened to me, and believed in the story before it ever reached the page.

To my daughters — you are the brightest parts of my story. Your love, patience, and laughter have carried me through more than you'll ever know. Thank you for forgiving my imperfections and loving me anyway.

To my family — thank you for loving me through every chapter of this life. Your presence, grace, and humor gave me the strength to keep going.

To Kathy and Larry — thank you for opening your home to me after the accident, and for continuing to support me throughout my life. You gave me safety, stability, and love — and even introduced me to Doug. I will never forget what you've given me.

To Robyn, Paula, and Lorry — what began as friendship became sisterhood. You stood beside me through the hardest chapters and the healing ones. We laughed, cried, and rebuilt together, piece by piece.

To Jacki — thank you for nudging me gently, and persistently, to put my story down in words. Your encouragement lit the spark that became this book.

To Doug — thank you for reading every emotional word with the patience of a saint, for editing with a sharp eye and a full heart, and for picking up the slack at home so I could write. This book is ours in more ways than one.

And to every reader who picks up these pages — thank you. If ever one sentence helps you feel less alone, more seen, or more hopeful, then every hard-earned word was worth it.

Reading Group Questions

1. Lennie's story begins with the warmth of home and the rhythm of a loving family. How did her early experiences shape your understanding of what was lost later in the book?

2. The memoir traces a journey through trauma, silence, and reconnection. How did Lennie's voice evolve over time — and when did you first feel her beginning to reclaim it?

3. Shame, secrecy, and strength are all woven into this story. Were there moments that surprised you with their emotional impact? Why do you think those scenes stood out?

4. Gathering the Pieces is a title that speaks to both brokenness and healing. What pieces do you think Lennie had gathered by the end? Are there pieces you've gathered in your own life?

5. Memoirs often ask the question: What does it mean to survive? How does Lennie's survival redefine strength? Did her story challenge or affirm your view of resilience?

6. Several key relationships shift throughout the memoir — with sisters, daughters, romantic partners, and self. Which relationship arc moved you the most, and why?

7. There are moments of unexpected humor, warmth, and connection, even amid heartbreak. Was there a scene that made you smile when you least expected it?

8. Silence plays a powerful role in Lennie's story. What kinds of silence were present — protective, harmful, healing? How did those silences change over time?

9. By the end of the memoir, Lennie's life looks radically different from where it began. What inner transformations made that possible?
10. If you could ask the author one question, what would it be?

About the Author

Lennie Campbell is a natural storyteller with a heart full of hope and a voice shaped by experience. A devoted mother, resilient survivor, and gentle guide, she shares her journey with honesty, grace, and the kind of wisdom that comes only from living through life's hardest moments.

In Gathering the Pieces, Lennie opens the door to her past not only to reflect, but also to offer comfort, connection, and courage to others finding their way forward. She wrote this memoir to remind readers that they are never truly alone. No matter how broken life may feel, healing is possible—and every piece of your story matters.

Today, Lennie lives in Hawai'i, where the slower pace of life, the rhythm of the ocean, and the spirit of Aloha remind her daily of what truly matters: family, connection, and living with an open heart.

For Those Still Gathering

If you're walking through grief...
you're not alone.

If you've been silenced...
your voice still waits.

If you've lost someone...
love still holds.

And even if you've lost yourself along the way—
you can still gather the pieces.

Let's Stay Connected

Thank you for reading Gathering the Pieces.

If my story touched something in you,
I'd love to stay in touch.

You can visit:
www.GatheringThePieces.com

to sign up for weekly inspirational messages or leave a
memory sentence on the Lantern Page — a gentle, sacred
space to honor someone you've loved and lost.

You can also reach me by email at:
Lennie@GatheringThePieces.com

And follow along on Facebook:
@LennieCampbellAuthor

We heal in pieces.
We connect one story at a time.

www.ingramcontent.com/pod-product-compliance
Lightning Source LLC
Chambersburg PA
CBHW060124130626
46556CB00006B/2223